Dear Reader,

Hello and Welcome to Firing Up Imagination: Practical Ideas for Parent and Child Enjoyment over Consumerism and Advertising.

Now that I've covered the necessary legal formalities, I'd like you to please enjoy this book. I'm sorry that I had to start the book in such a way, but now you can go on to feel and work with this book.

Firing Up Imagination:
Practical Ideas for Parent and Child Enjoyment over Consumerism and Advertising

© Philip J. Taylor Ph.D.

INTRODUCTION- A Soul Enriching Program To Improve And Enhance Communication With Your Child

This book is dedicated to healthy living ways. If attention, prevention, and meaningful intervention can help children succeed with their parents love and support, then we can go hand-in-hand to live more today and anticipate a better tomorrow. So I share life experiences with you and would like to get you thinking and inquiring about the thousand-and-one bright ideas you have up your sleeve to conjure up all your dreams. Activities, tools, methods, story clips, humour, and techniques to bring you and your child closer together are all employed to tease out your individual and collective creative streaks.

The first Chapter introduces you and your family as consumers who are endowed with economic muscle. The second Chapter challenges you and your child with practical pointers to engage in a stimulating array of activities that bring morals, choices, and fun into play with guidelines for virtually each day of the month. The third Chapter gets you actively involved in developing school and community events that bring awareness and education for consumerist understanding, reflection, and action in your school or community. The fourth Chapter provides you more ideas, activities, brainwaves to spark family involvements with healthy growth. The fifth Chapter deals with decisions you make with your children about suitable, sound, safe, and exciting choices. The sixth Chapter throws light on background information on people, education, power, profits that surround advertising.

The aim of this book, as I've pointed out in the seventh Chapter, is to inspire you and give you practical suggestions that might lead you to your bank of resources that support "The Revitalisation of Daily Living".

"There's enough on this planet for everyone's needs but not for everyone's greed."

Mahatma Gandhi

FORWARD–"THE MAGIC IS WITHIN YOU"

You are now reading a book that I hope will change your life. Interested? Take a minute to listen to my story. I wrote it for you

When I was a child I played in the backyard, the fields of Alicedale (named for the late Princess Alice, the cousin of the Queen of England, who actually once visited with a neighbour and sipped tea with the family in the 1950s. The Mallam's home). I visited and revisited with old neighbours 'Kia and 'Tiema Mallam, Pamela, Louis Abrahams, and my sister Linda. For the Christmas fare as in childhood the table was laden with goodies and admonishments of "eat, eat, have some more". All they needed to add was, don't be shy (a familiar and requisite urging of parents to let the reins open on the eat fest during the festive season) Athlone, Cape Town, South Africa. We lived in an attractive stuccoed sturdy council house filled with lovely memories and had what we needed.

No television, books aplenty, newspapers, lots of radio time, and hours spent in libraries wherever I could find them. The wide outdoors of South Africa was where my friends and I found our playgrounds. In the purple blue Table Mountain, vast beaches of the warm Indian Ocean and the cooler Atlantic, and wild life game preserves at Cape Point, the Garden Route. It would be quite ludicrous to imagine that we lived the lifestyles of the rich and famous. It simply was that nature was free and we took advantage of every chance we could get during school holidays to thoroughly drink up South Africa's wondrous fauna, flora, sights, and fresh air. Imagination, creativity, resourcefulness, and fun and laughter played an enormous part in helping to overcome the odds.

In fact even as South Africa now undergoes the joys and pains of democratization, the world well knows South Africa was once a society wracked by the cruelty and violence of apartheid or racial discrimination. I lived in South Africa during the years 1947-1970. When I lived there I never wanted to become an educator. I wanted to be educated. However, because of the colour of my skin I wasn't granted my wish to become a chemical engineer. So I pursued other avenues. My education and my life stem from my parents' knowledge that education was the only way to survive.

Thus, after many years of study and research I did doctoral research and dedicated the past thirty years of my life to the pursuit of education. I feel deeply that all the children in my country of birth and all the children of the world have the right and opportunity to education that makes a better life for themselves and their families and their countries. As a former South African now a citizen of Canada, I am also able to bring my life as a Canadian and citizen of the world to bear upon this book. So, it is also dedicated to the ongoing challenge to reconstruct cherished foundations of human freedom–freedom, based on the belief in a non-racial democracy as a possibility with strong families and supportive people and institutions at the heart of sensitive democracies. If it has succeeded in even raising questions about the corrupting nature of absolute power, then it has achieved its goal in opening minds to not wanting to visit the place of past oppression of any colour or stripe again. Hope you and your child have fun with it too!

LET'S FLASH FORWARD TO TODAY.

Don Massey a business associate and mentor once said, "The information age, as we call it, has always been at the finger tips of those willing to read." I cannot but say again that I spent hours in local libraries when I was not in school, on the sports field playing soccer, cricket, or rugby, or working in the garden or doing chores at home or a bob-a-job stint for my local Boy Scouts Cub's group. Like the fast food craze, there is a clamouring today for quick concise information. Specific markets devour information so soon as it is produced.

Since it is relatively EASY to develop and present information, why not find out how you can learn, help others, enjoy family life more, and make a decent living from this "newly minted" need for greater self-sufficiency and accountability in your life?

After teaching for thirty years I was able to go on a pre-retirement program that gives me the freedom to teach part time and work as an educational consultant and information provider. I'm having loads of fun.

Like my friendship with books and information in the libraries of Athlone and Canada, I want to share with you. Please walk with me and let's hold hands. Let's see if this book can unlock the magic within you that leads to your success. When the children of the world all succeed then we go forward as a civilization dedicated to fair play for all human beings. Practice clear thinking, sound family and money management practices, grow a climate of non-violence, and besides unlock new possibilities to interact with your child in new and creative ways that turn the key into breathless pools of imagination that nourishes a warm, caring, and supportive home, school, and community.

Your Consumer Power: Taking Action

"Allow yourself to be a torch and allow the flame of your torch to be transmitted to other torches. Practising like that, you can help peace and joy grow in the entire world."

Thich Nhat Hanh

WHERE'S THE WIZARD'S WAND–WHEN IT'S NOT IN MY WALLET? IN ADVERTISING? IT'S EVERYWHERE.

No, it's not your imagination. The amount of advertising and marketing North Americans are exposed to daily has exploded over the past decade; studies show, that on average we see 3,000 ads per day. At the gas pumps, in the movie theatre, in a washroom stall, during sporting events–advertising is impossible to avoid. Even outer space isn't safe from commercialization: the Russian space program launched a rocket bearing a 30-foot

Pizza Hut logo, and some companies have investigated placing ads in space that will be visible from earth. The challenge of the future may be finding public and private spaces that are free of advertising. What would you want to see more of in your space? Were you to make a wish list of 5 images you'd want to see more of, what would they remind you? What place would they occupy in your life? Marketers are pressed to find even more innovative and aggressive ways to cut through the "ad clutter" or "ad fatigue" of modern life.

Here's an overview of some of the ways marketers are targeting us:

Ambient advertising

Cars, bicycles, taxis and buses have become moving commercials. Ambient ads appear on store floors, at gas pumps, in washrooms stalls, on elevator walls, park benches, telephones, fruit and even pressed into the sand on beaches. With the cost of traditional media advertising skyrocketing and a glut of ads fighting for consumers' attention, marketers are aggressively seeking out new advertising vehicles.

Stealth-endorsers

The trend now is to brand celebrities with specific merchandise by having them use or wear products in public appearances or promote them in media interviews—without making it clear that the celebrities are paid spokespeople.

Naming rights

Corporations are turning public spaces into commodities by purchasing naming rights to arenas, theatres, parks, schools, museums and even subway systems. Cash-strapped municipalities see naming rights as a way to raise much-needed revenues without raising taxes.

Hope for children's media from the Joan Ganz Cooney Center

Children's hospital not "selling" naming rights, just naming new trauma center after the company that donated $10 million.

BREAKING: Children's hospital naming rights go to… Abercrombie & Fitch?

Nationwide Children's Hospital in Columbus, Ohio is considering giving naming rights for its new emergency department to Abercrombie & Fitch.

You read that right.

You know, a hospital? Where they care about children's health? A lot? And you know, Abercrombie 'n' Fitch? Where they don't so much?

See, in the Abercrombie 'n' Fitch world, the sexualization of young girls leads to fun, fun, more fun, and then, happiness! And not to depression, eating disorders, and sexual problems when they become adults.

You may remember the A 'n' F little-girl-thong fiasco? CEO Mike Jeffries, in a Salon interview, says he thinks that the thongs made for middle-school girls with "Wink Wink" and "Eye Candy" printed on them were "cute!"

"People said we were cynical, that we were sexualizing little girls. But you know what? I still think those are cute underwear for little girls. And I think anybody who gets on a bandwagon about thongs for little girls is crazy…"

Ohhhhh-kay. The interview continues:

…when I ask him how important sex and sexual attraction are in what he calls the "emotional experience" he creates for his customers, he says, "It's almost everything. That's why we hire good-looking people in our stores. Because good-looking people attract other good-looking people, and we want to market to cool, good-looking people. We don't market to anyone other than that."

I wonder if that would go for the children's emergency room, too.

Parents for Ethical Marketing, along with 15 other advocacy organizations and about 800 Ph.D.s have signed on to a CCFC letter asking Nationwide Children's Hospital not to sell the naming rights to Abercrombie 'n' Fitch.

Information on where to sign on to the request will follow.

Related from Bob Garfield: **Abercrombie Underwear Shop Plays Up Goods, But Not Its Own**

This entry was posted on Tuesday, March 11, 2008 at 4:45 pm and is filed under Retailers, The Problem. You can follow any responses to this entry through the RSS 2.0 feed. You can leave a response, or trackback from your own site (Naming Rights 2008).

Targeted advertising

LITTLEST PET SHOP VIPs (Bunny) Enter the virtual LITTLEST PET SHOP world with your very own VIP pet bunny. Find your pet's secret code hidden in its collar–and then visit www.littlestpetshop.com to unlock exclusive games, activities and lots of other cool surprises that you can play with your virtual pet pal! Snuggle your plush pet while you play online. Now you've got even more ways to add to the pet-lovin' fun! Cute-as-a-bunny plush pet has a hidden code that lets you play with a virtual version of your pet online and discover all kinds of cool activities for even more pet-lovin' fun!

(Hasbro 2008).

Targeted ads are a form of Internet marketing. Using sophisticated data collecting technologies, Web sites can combine a user's personal information with surfing preferences to create ads that are specifically tailored for that user.

Cross-merchandizing

A wave of media mergers over the past decade has produced a handful of integrated companies. For example, when the world's largest entertainment conglomerate AOL Time Warner was preparing the release of the film Harry Potter and the Sorcerer's Stone, it enlisted all its various media divisions–cable systems, specialty channels, TV networks, magazines and Internet companies–to help mass-market the movie and the spin-off merchandise.

Product placement

The future of product placement as a successful advertising tool was assured when the 1982 film ET featured Reese's Pieces in a pivotal scene–causing sales of the candy to jump 65 per cent. Since that time, product placement in movies, on TV, and increasingly in video games, has become a commonplace marketing strategy (Palmieri 2007).

How Marketers Target Kids

Kids represent an important demographic to marketers because they have their own purchasing power, they influence their parents' buying decisions and they're the adult consumers of the future.

Industry spending on advertising to children has exploded in the past decade, increasing from a mere $100 million in 1990 to more than $2 billion in 2000.

Digital or "virtual" advertising

Digital advertising goes one step further than product placement by using computer technology to add products to scenes that were never there at the beginning. This practice is common in sporting events coverage, where ads are digitally inserted onto the billboards, sideboards and playing surfaces in arenas and stadiums.

Parents today are willing to buy more for their kids because trends such as smaller family size, dual incomes and postponing children until later in life mean that families have more disposable income. As well, guilt can play a role in spending decisions as time-stressed parents substitute material goods for time spent with their kids.

Here are some of the strategies marketers employ to target children and teens:

Pester Power

"We're relying on the kid to pester the mom to buy the product, rather than going straight to the mom."

Barbara A. Martino, Advertising Executive

Today's kids have more autonomy and decision-making power within the family than in previous generations, so it follows that kids are vocal about what they want their parents to buy. "**Pester power**" refers to children's ability to nag their parents into purchasing items they may not otherwise buy. Marketing to children is all about creating pester power, because advertisers know what a powerful force it can be.

According to the 2001 marketing industry book Kidfluence, pestering or nagging can be divided into two categories–"persistence" and "importance." **Persistence nagging** (a plea, that is repeated over and over again) is not as effective as the more sophisticated "**importance nagging**." This latter method appeals to parents' desire to provide the best for their children, and plays on any guilt they may have about not having enough time for their kids.

The marriage of psychology and marketing

To effectively market to children, advertisers need to know what makes kids tick. With the help of well-paid researchers and psychologists, advertisers now have access to in-depth knowledge about children's developmental, emotional and social needs at different ages. Using research that analyzes children's behaviour, fantasy lives, art work, even their dreams, companies are able to craft sophisticated marketing strategies to reach young people.

The issue of using child psychologists to help marketers target kids gained widespread public attention in 1999, when a group of U.S. mental health professionals issued a public letter to the American Psychological Association (APA) urging them to declare the practice unethical. The APA is currently studying the issue.

Building brand name loyalty

Canadian author Naomi Klein tracks the birth of "brand" marketing in her 2000 book No Logo. According to Klein, the mid-1980s saw the birth of a new kind of corporation–Nike, Calvin Klein, Tommy Hilfiger, to name a few–which changed their primary corporate focus from producing products to creating an image for their brand name. By moving their manufacturing operations to countries with cheap labour, they freed up money to create their powerful marketing messages. It has been a tremendously profitable formula, and has led to the creation of some of the most wealthy and powerful multi-national corporations the world has seen.

Marketers plant the seeds of brand recognition in very young children, in the hopes that the seeds will grow into lifetime relationships. According to the Center for a New American Dream, babies as young as six months of age can form mental images of corporate logos and mascots. Brand loyalties can be established as early as age two, and by the time children head off to school most can recognize hundreds of brand logos.

> "Brand marketing must begin with children. Even if a child does not buy the product and will not for many years... the marketing must begin in childhood."
>
> James McNeal, The Kids Market, 1999

While fast food, toy and clothing companies have been cultivating brand recognition in children for years, adult-oriented businesses such as banks and automakers are now getting in on the act.

Magazines such as Time, Sports Illustrated and People have all launched kid and teen editions–which boast ads for adult related products such as minivans, hotels and airlines.

Buzz or street marketing

The challenge for marketers is to cut through the intense advertising clutter in young people's lives. Many companies are using "buzz marketing"– a new twist on the tried-and-true "word of mouth" method. The idea is to find the coolest kids in a community and have them use or wear your product in order to create a buzz around it. Buzz, or "street marketing," as it's also called, can help a company to successfully connect with the savvy and elusive teen market by using trendsetters to give their products "cool" status.

Buzz marketing is particularly well-suited to the Internet, where young "Net promoters" use newsgroups, chat rooms and blogs to spread the word about music, clothes and other products among unsuspecting users.

Commercialization in education

School used to be a place where children were protected from the advertising and consumer messages that permeated their world—but not any more. Budget shortfalls are forcing school boards to allow corporations access to students in exchange for badly needed cash, computers and educational materials.

Corporations realize the power of the school environment for promoting their name and products. A school setting delivers a captive youth audience and implies the endorsement of teachers and the educational system. Marketers are eagerly exploiting this medium in a number of ways, including:

- Sponsored educational materials: for example, a Kraft "healthy eating" kit to teach about Canada's Food Guide (using Kraft products); or forestry company Canfor's primary lesson plans that make its business focus seem like environmental management rather than logging.
- Supplying schools with technology in exchange for high company visibility.
- Exclusive deals with fast food or soft drink companies to offer their products in a school or district.
- Advertising posted in classrooms, school buses, on computers, etc. in exchange for funds.
- Contests and incentive programs: for example, the Pizza Hut reading incentives program in which children receive certificates for free pizza if they achieve a monthly reading goal; or Campbell's Labels for Education project, in which

Campbell provides educational resources for schools in exchange for soup labels collected by students.

- Sponsoring school events: The Canadian company ShowBiz brings moveable video dance parties into schools to showcase various sponsors' products.

The Internet

The Internet is an extremely desirable medium for marketers wanting to target children:

- It's part of youth culture. This generation of young people is growing up with the Internet as a daily and routine part of their lives.
- Parents generally do not understand the extent to which kids are being marketed to online.
- Kids are often online alone, without parental supervision.
- Unlike broadcasting media, which have codes regarding advertising to kids, the Internet is unregulated.
- Sophisticated technologies make it easy to collect information from young people for marketing research, and to target individual children with personalized advertising.
- By creating engaging, interactive environments based on products and brand names, companies can build brand loyalties from an early age.

Marketing adult entertainment to kids

Children are often aware of and want to see entertainment meant for older audiences because it is actively marketed to them. In a report released in 2000, the U.S. Federal Trade Commission (FTC) revealed how the movie, music and video games industries routinely market violent entertainment to young children.

The FTC studied 44 films rated "Restricted," and discovered that 80 percent were targeted to children under 17. Marketing plans included TV commercials run during hours when young viewers were most likely to be watching. One studio's plan for a violent R-rated film stated, "Our goal was to find the elusive teen target audience, and make sure that everyone between the ages of 12 and 18 was exposed to the film."

Music containing "explicit-content" labels were targeted at young people through extensive advertising in the most popular teen venues on television, and radio, in print, and online.

Of the video game companies investigated for the report, 70 percent regularly marketed Mature rated games (for 17 years and older) to children. Marketing plans included placing advertising in media that would reach a substantial

BUT my husband is a shopaholic!

"My Husband Is a Shopaholic!"

Karen desperately wants Todd to curb his excessive spending habits but he can't seem to get a grip. Can this marriage be saved?

Her Turn

"We're in way over our heads," said Karen, 49, a paralegal. "Todd hasn't told me exactly how much debt we have–he handles our money and I don't like to probe–but I'm fielding daily calls from collection agencies. Yet last month he leased a new BMW for our daughter, Kim, 25. He can't stop himself–he just gives her money without bothering to check with me. We've never let her know how strapped we are, so she's happy to accept his generosity. And Todd just bought another antique watch to add to his.

He hides them all over the house—he thinks I don't know, but I do… (Rosen 2008).

SCORE BIG POINTS WITH SENSITIVE AND EFFECTIVE PARENTING SKILLS AND ATTITUDES WITH THE TOOLS THIS BOOK WILL PROVIDE YOU WITH MOVE AHEAD WITH –

How to Make Practical Ideas Work For Good Family Times And Enrich Precious Moments Spent Together?

Let's face it. From the kitchen, to the bathroom, to the bus, your car radio or MP3 player, iPod, computer, e-mail, ADVERTISING is a staple of the business world.

Do you think that we buy more things than we really need each day? Make an estimate of things, which your family would normally spend money on each day for: food, gas, bus fare, clothing etc.?

Do you think your family could go for a whole day without spending any money? Making the difference between wants, needs, desires, and the advertiser's pull on our lives is an essential first step towards making effective decisions as parents, consumers, children, and citizens wanting to get a better grip on our lives and purchasing or buying powers. Buying for the sake of simply answering manufactured, false, or unwanted goods and services is called consumerism.

What is Consumerism?

CONSUMERISM IS A PATTERN OF BEHAVIOUR that helps to destroy our environment, personal financial health, the common good of individuals and human institutions. Mass media perpetuates the myth of consumerism as a priority of the New Capitalism. As America settles into its nightly routine of television viewing, corporate profiteers are quick to substitute the lure of material luxury and consumer gratification for the fading spirit. Media advertising sells an image–an empty shell. Corporate America placates its flaccid public with dispiriting pastiche. There is only fraudulent illusion. Instead of Swiss clockworks encased in hand carved hardwood, the consumer is offered a cheap imitation of routed particleboard and computer chip technology. Who cares as long as it looks good? (Cronk 1996).

How can you save more money, work less and lead a more satisfying life? What can you do to save our environments from consumerist superexploitation of peoplekind's common human heritage natural and human resources?

In becoming more aware of such issues it is important for you to feel and see ways that you can become a part of the solution as a better informed citizen for a more equitable way of life where you live and the world over- thinking locally and acting globally is the key to unlocking our individual and collective consciousness that **CAN HELP TO ERADICATE** poverty, injustice, discrimination, violence, hunger, and disease. In this process you also realize your powers of one who is educated enough to take on seemingly overwhelming odds that are imposed on you by governments, corporations, profiteers, and unthinking or heartless officialdom.

Business Week Attacks Microlending in Mexico

Business Week has devoted significant space to a Keith Epstein and Geri Smith article that attacks "The Ugly Side of Microlending."

Microlending has received a great deal of attention recently, most of it positive, as it has enabled poor entrepeneurs in developing countries to generate income and even build real wealth.

However, Epstein and Smith highlight the predatory nature of Latin American microlending. They focus on Banco Azteca, a fast-growing Latin American bank generating "a torrent of revenue" from microlending in Mexico. In addition, Banamex (Citigroup) and HSBC are angling in on the action.

[The poor] will pay interest rates most Americans would consider outrageous, if not usurious... With no legal limits on interest levels and little government oversight, for-profit banks **in Mexico impose annual interest rates on poor borrowers**

that typically range from 50% to 120%. That compares with a worldwide average of 31% among nonprofit m i c r o - l e n d i n g institutions, and the 22% to 29% that

Americans with bad credit histories incur on credit-card debt.

What is interesting about the article is that while hammering Mexican microlending, Epstein and Smith completely ignore the obvious analogy of payday loans in the U.S.

The Scourge of Payday Loans

What is a "Payday Loan"?

Borrowers visit a payday lending store and secure a small cash loan, usually in the range of $100 to $500 with payment in full due at the borrower's next paycheck (usually a two week term). Finance charges on payday loans are typically in the range of $15 to $30 per $100 borrowed for the two-week period, which translates to **rates ranging from 390 percent to 780 percent** when expressed as an annual percentage rate (APR)[4]. The borrower writes a check to the lender in the full amount of the loan plus fees. On the maturity date, the borrower is expected to return to the store to repay the loan in person. If the borrower doesn't repay the loan in person, the lender may process the check traditionally or through electronic withdrawal from the borrower's checking account…

I thought usury and loan-sharking were both illegal, but that's apparently not the case.

…most states have usury laws which forbid interest rates in excess of a certain APR. **Payday lenders have succeeded in getting around usury laws in some states by forming relationships with banks chartered in a different state with no usury ceiling (such as South Dakota or Delaware).** This practice has been referred to as "Rate exportation", the "agency model" and the "rent-a-bank" model…

Put simply, payday loans appear far more exploitive than the practice of microlending. That Epstein and Smith ignore this simple comparison is at best puzzling, but more likely indicative of an unspoken agenda (Directorblue 2007).

"Poverty in the world is an artificial creation;
it does not belong to human civilization. We
can change it."

"Poor people are not asking for charity; charity
is not a solution for poverty."

"Only thing we need to do soon, redesign our
institution and policies. People can change their own life provided
they got the right kind of institutional support."

Dr. Muhammad Yunus

It is worth our time to see how these movements basically evolved with the following summary.

President Obama (then Senator Obama) said that as President, he will double the funding for the Consumer Product Safety Commission, and make sure it has the inspectors it needs to ensure that the goods we're buying are safe. Obama is committed to expanding the agency's regulatory powers, and helping them respond quickly and efficiently when they're alerted to a problem to prevent more children from injury or death (p. 1). "Today, going Christmas shopping isn't just a matter of what toys would bring our children the most joy, but what toys are safe to give them," Obama said (Obama 2007).

In 1962 President Kennedy enunciated the now famous Consumer Bill of Rights: 1) the right to safety, 2) the right to be informed, 3) the right to choose, and 4) the right to be heard. These are rights with which we would not disagree. The question is really one of what we do in the name of these rights, for these are the rights only of a truly free society. What President Kennedy did not say, and which is more to the point, is that the right to safety is appropriate only in the exercise of reasonable and prudent judgment by the consumer.

The right to be informed carries with it the responsibility of becoming better educated. The right to choose carries with it the opportunity of making the kind of choice which consumer protection-ism prohibits. And the right to be heard carries with it a respect for the differing desires and wants of one's fellow men (Brunk 1972). Speaking of balance, on his first meeting with Armstrong, Jacki Byard said, "As I watched him and talked with him, I felt he was the most natural man. Playing, talking, singing, he was so perfectly natural the tears came to my eyes" (Gottlieb, 1996, p.1041).

Advertising daily deluges our children and what can we do to transform the corporate view of them as "targets"? I tackle some 'Special Issues for Young Children, Special Issues for Tweens and Teens, GETTING INVOLVED, Understanding Advertising Guidelines and Codes, Dealing with Marketing, and What we can do as caring and guiding Parents to guide children's buying decisions.

Taking Action

To Gain Popular Support

Taking a closer clinical look at those consumer issues which have gained widespread public support in recent years, we can perhaps gain some appreciation of the characteristics of such issues and their applicability to our food supply. First, the social benefits of an issue must be easily rationalized usually by some grossly oversimplified cause and effect relationship: for example, the directed rationale in truth-in-lending, truth-in-packaging, informative labeling and so on. Benefits must be directed at a major proportion of consumers and the more such benefits have the appearance of being directed at health or economic welfare the more viable the issue. Typical of popular consumer issues is that costs of protection are hidden by dispersion throughout a complex production and distribution industry; or such costs are easily, though sometimes spuriously, rationalized as falling on large, concentrated or prosperous industries.

One of the remarkable features of the marketing system, as contrasted with the negativism involved in many consumer issues, is the way it has broadened choice in serving the specific and diverse needs of an almost endless number of consumer groups each having peculiar requirements. We must not make the mistake of assuming a universality of consumer values. Each of us, in terms of his own individual values, tends to rationalize what he considers appropriate universal values for others. We have difficulty understanding and respecting values other than our own. Said another way in the words of Teddy Wilson:

"Every musician, no matter how good, usually has something out of balance. But in [Louis] Armstrong everything was in balance. He had no weak point. I don't think there's been a musician since Armstrong, who has had all the factors in balance; all the factors were equally developed" (Gottlieb, 1999, p.1041).

References

Brunk, M. (1972). A talk before the Annual Meeting of the Cooperative Extension Association of Livingston County, New York, November 15, The Freeman, The Foundation for Economic Education, Inc., February 1973, 23, 2.

Cronk, R. (1996). Consumerism and the New Capitalism. Retrieved March 31, 2010 from http://www.westland.net/Venice/art/cronk/consumer.htm

Digital advertising. Retrieved June 25, 2005 from http://www.media-awareness.ca/english/parents/marketing/advertising_everywhere.cfm

Epstein, K. & Smith, G. The Ugly Side of Microlending.Business Week, 4064, D24, pp.38-44. (The Ugly Side of Microlending) Business Week attacks Microlending in Mexico http://directorblue.blogspot.com/2007/12/microlending-in-mexico-and-payday-loans.html Retrieved July 20, 2008.

Gottlieb, R. (1996). Reading Jazz: A Gathering*News Release p.9 of Autobiography, Reportage, and Criticism from 1919 to Now. New York: Vintage Books.

Hanh, T. (2004). Taming The Tiger Within: Meditations on Transforming Difficult Emotions. New York: Riverhead Books.

HASBRO http://www.hasbro.com/default.cfm?page=browse&product_id=21063 Retrieved October 16, 2008.

Naming Rights http://www.parentsforethicalmarketing.org/blog/2008/03/11/breaking-childrens-hospital-naming-rights-go-to-abercrombie-fitch/bercrombie & Fitch?" Retrieved July 21, 2008.

Obama. Vows to Protect Children from Lead-Based Toys, Des Moines, IA | December 15, 2007; Unveils Plan to Strengthen Consumer Product Safety Commission http://www.barackobama.com/2007/12/15/obama_vows_to_protect_children.php Retrieved November 14, 2008, pp. 1-2.

Palmeri, C. (2007). Hasbro's Little Cash Cows.Business Week, D24, p.66. Nielsen http://www.nielsen.com/media/2007/pr_071211a_download.pdf Retrieved July 10, 2008

Rosen, M. http://lifestyle.msn.com/relationships/articlelhj.aspx?cp-documentid=8319170 Retrieved July 25, 2008, My Husband Is a Shopaholic!

Yunus, M. & Weber, K. (2007). Creating a World Without Poverty: Social Business and the Future of Capitalism. New York: Public Affairs.

Activities To Go

"We were all put in this Garden on Planet Earth to serve and love the divine in us all and in higher powers greater than ourselves. "The Creator has a master plan He's got wonders for everyone, and oohhhhhhhhh…"

Leon Thomas

PRACTICAL IDEAS

1. Growing in the garden of self sufficiency

In the backyard garden or a city botanical garden, a riverside everglade, a swamp, a forest, a jungle, an arboretum, and so on.

Who: Children K-Adult
When: Off (indoor greenhouses, rock gardens, plants, or nature study venues) and on season definitely outdoors in fair or foul weather.

© Knysnaforesttours 2008

Where: Outdoors, indoors, hydroponics, bottles, rooftops, cellars for fungus, under rocks, seaside etc.

Gardening is an art science and source of sore backs and great contentment for most adults. What do you like about gardening and what happens when your seeds don't grow? How do you feel? Do you just give up? Do you imagine what will grow?

What: Plan the layout of the garden and make a list of the materials and equipment you'll need to get the job started and maintain a healthy garden Plant the seed of an idea now

In the **Kingdom of the Golden Dragon** By Isabel Allende, for instance, for grade 5-8 students an exciting adventure is unraveled when the-Buddhist monk Tensing and his disciple, Prince Dil Bahadur, are journeying through the Himalayan peaks in search of healing plants when they come face to face with a tribe of once-fierce Yetis. These legendary half-human, half-ape monsters inhabit a lush valley heated by thermal pools and hot springs and are unaware that it's the toxic minerals in the water that has weakened them and slowed their rate of reproduction. Meanwhile, 16-year-old Alexander Cold; his intrepid writer/ explorer grandmother, Kate; and his soul mate, Nadia Santos, daughter of the guide who led Kate and Alex on their previous expedition into the South American rain forest, described in City of the Beasts (Harper Collins, 2002 CITY), are off on a new International Geographic expedition (Amazon, 2008).

2. Fairy Tales

Set your course by imagining your authorship or creation of some new idea, feeling, power, service, or product that does something to make the life of someone you know get better. Make it a fairy tale in which you decide on: Ideas, Title, Plot, Setting, Main Characters, Resolution, and Final Sentence. This format can be adapted according to the

level of your children and the complexity you want to have in planning a narrative. To honour the place of First Nations and traditional storytelling you might also want to look at the First Nation's Garden at the Montreal Botannical Gardens or another beautiful garden near to where you live, get into making snowshoes, try learning the Thunderhawk Mohawk Dance, basket weaving skills and the story of Winoosis by Christine Sioui Wawanoloath, artist and author Abenaki-Wendat.

Harry Potter's Charm

This truly is a rags-to-riches tale of a welfare Mom who made it big with her creative genius. I find so fascinating her journey to sharing her life with children and her daily writing regime to get her best out there for children to enjoy. Her phenomenal success is no less awesome to me as well.

HARRY POTTER IN CHINA

Globalization, Consumerism, and Cultural Change in Modern China

Introduction: The Harry Potter books, by British author J.K. Rowling, are the most popular children's fantasy books in publishing history. In the US alone, there is one copy in print for nearly every 2.5 Americans. The fifth book in the series became the first English-Language book ever to top the bestseller list in France. Since the first book was published 10 years ago the series has sold over 400 million copies world wide and has been translated into 64 languages. Indeed, "Pottermania" has crossed national and cultural boundaries and become a truly  global phenomenon. Even in China, where many critics thought the books too foreign to gain wide acceptance, the Harry Potter series has set publishing records and drawn millions of urban Chinese youth into the orbit of global popular culture.

Jonathan Henderson Parental vs. Corporate Influence

Amy Jussel (2006) in observing the state of crass consumerism pitched at youth noted:

Wal-Mart is leading the techno-begging frenzy with a whimsically cheerful interactive toyland site of smarmy back-talking elves with attitude. These obnoxiously sassy lil' fellas spurt out kid-speak like, "puhhhleeeze" and "very funny…NOT!" Is there really a need to further incentivize annoying voices? Po Wal-Mart Elves: Crass Commercialism, Interactive 'Tude' (p.1).

Power shopping prepubescents? Cartoon icons that talk with 'tude?

4. Kids not only want things, but also have acquired the socially sanctioned right to want—a right which parents are loath to violate. Layered onto direct child enticement and the supposed autonomy of the child-consumer are the day-to-day circumstances of overworked parents: a daily barrage of requests, tricky financial negotiations, and that nagging, unspoken desire to build the life/style they have learned to want during their childhoods (Dan Cook, 2001).

There might not be anything apparently wrong with businesses trying to make sales and profit. However, the effects of things like mass consumption, the intense advertising, and targeting to children and its emphasis over so many aspects of daily lives is of concern. That is, the effects of constantly buying things, while discarding older but often functioning things, increasing demands on the world's resources for this consumption, managing more waste, exploiting other people to labor over this, and so on. And all this while many still go hungry and poor because their lands are being used to export away food and other resources for producing products to be consumed elsewhere. It is in this way that the pressure and drive for profits has led to an over-commercialized consumerism, which has wider effects around the world and on the unseen majority peoples of the world, as we look at next.

According to Naud (2008), to reduce the stresses that parents often feel when trying to keep up with the growing demands of their children, Zelt says teaching delayed gratification to teens is helpful. For instance if their teen says he or she has to have the latest gadget, ask them to wait a week to s Brand hungry teens benefit from value lessons

Parents urged to teach delayed gratification and wait a week to see if they still want it (p. 2).

Parents have a hard time providing guidance and influence on their children when there are so many conflicting influences from outside: Positive Parenting Values and Strategies and Place of Elders in Children's Lives & Finding Meaning for Troubled Times.

- What were their issues?
- How did they handle them?
- What successes did they achieve?
- What were shortcomings
- Thoughts of The Depression of the 1929 [(lifestyles of a vanished childhood (jacket) Images of childhood in William McPherson's novel, Testing The Current, 1984.

4. Freedom and the Great Global Robbery of Childhood

Commercialization of childhood itself, of festivals etc. and the commercialization of public and religious holidays help promote sales as well. Christmas time in numerous countries, such as the United States, sees a very high amount of consumerism. The toy industry for example depends on Christmas quite a lot. The promotion of St. Nicholas/Santa Claus/Father Christmas and an almost benign factory (or workshop) of elves and so forth producing toys for free was a boost to commercialize Christmas, especially for children. What of Diwali, Tet, Chinese New Year, Eid, Hunnukah, and all the major world faiths, cultures, religions, and traditions?

Find Gordon Biggs and then go on with your life. Find the villains and then make wise choices (a board game (with rules for fairness for all) based on the London Great Train Robbery and Daring Escape to Brazil, Eventual Capture, Trail, and Guilty Verdict, and Extradition?)

5. Child consumerism seen from the lure of materialism

Special Issues for Tweens and Teens and The "Tween Market"

"The entertainment companies… look at the teen market as part of this massive empire they're colonizing. (Robert McChesney, The Merchants of Cool, 2000). One of the most important recent developments in advertising to kids has been the defining of a 'tween' market (ages 8 to 12). No longer little children, and not yet teens, tweens are starting to develop their sense of identity and are anxious to cultivate a sophisticated self-image. And marketers are discovering there's lots of money to be made by treating tweens like teenagers. The marketing industry is forcing tweens to grow up quickly. Industry research reveals that children 11 and older don't consider themselves children anymore. The Toy Manufacturers of America have changed their target market from birth to 14, to birth to ten years of age.

A 2000 report from the Federal Trade Commission in the U.S. revealed how Hollywood routinely recruits tweens (some as young as nine) to evaluate its story concepts, commercials, theatrical trailers and rough cuts for R-rated movies. By treating pre-adolescents as independent, mature consumers, marketers have been very successful in removing the gatekeepers (**parents**) from the picture–leaving tweens vulnerable to potentially unhealthy messages about body image, sexuality, relationships and violence.

Marketing "cool" to teens

Corporations capitalize on the age-old insecurities and self-doubts of teens by making them believe that to be truly cool, you need their product. According to No Logo author Naomi Klein, in the 1990s corporations discovered that the youth market was able and willing to pay top dollar in order to be "cool." The corporations have been chasing the elusive cool factor ever since.

Some companies hire "cool hunters" or "cultural spies" to infiltrate the world of teens and bring back the latest trends. Trying to stay ahead of the next trend can be a tricky business however, as cultural critic Douglas Rushkoff explains. "The minute a cool trend is discovered, repackaged, and sold to kids at the mall–it's no longer cool. So the kids turn to something else, and the whole process starts all over again." Teen anger, activism and attitude have become commodities that marketers co-opt, package and then sell back to teens. It's getting harder to tell what came first: youth culture, or the marketed version of youth culture. Does the media reflect today's teens, or are today's teens influenced by media portrayals of young people? It's important that parents discuss these issues with their teens, and challenge the materialistic values promoted in the media.

Body image and advertising

It's difficult for teens to develop healthy attitudes towards sexuality and body image when much of the advertising aimed at them is filled with images of impossibly thin, fit, beautiful and highly sexualized young people. The underlying marketing message is that there is a link between physical beauty and sex appeal–and popularity success, and happiness.

Fashion marketers such as Calvin Klein, Abercrombie & Fitch and Guess use provocative marketing campaigns featuring young models. These ads are selling more than clothing to teens–they're also selling adult sexuality.

Studies show that while teens received most of their information about sex from the media: magazines, TV, the Web, radio and movies, the majority say their parents shape their sexual decisions most, so it's important that parents talk to their kids about healthy sexuality, and about exploitive media images.

Media images can contribute to feelings of body-hatred and

self-loathing that can fuel eating problems. While body image has long been considered a female issue, an increasing number of boys now also suffer from eating disorders. A 1998 Health Canada survey on the health of Canadian youth noted that by grade ten, over three-quarters of the girls and one half of the boys surveyed said there they weren't happy with their bodies.

ARE THERE WAYS THAT YOU CAN HELP YOURSELF OUT OF THE CONSUMERIST TRAP?

7. Making Capitalism hum

How Marketers Target Kids

U.S. Toy Industry Sales Generate $22 Billion in 2007, says NPD Group NPD Group - February 12, 2008

The NPD Group reports that U.S. retail sales of toys generated $22.1 billion in 2007, compared to $22.6 billion in 2006, a decline of only 2 percent, despite the toy industry recalls and difficult economic conditions that plagued the industry in 2007.

The strong performance of two key super-categories helped to offset losses. Sales of Action Figures & Accessories were up 8 percent over 2006, while Vehicles experienced a 6 percent increase over the same time period.

The most significant losses were experienced in Infant/Preschool, Outdoor & Sports Toys, and Dolls with respective declines of 5 percent, 5 percent and 8 percent.

Top properties for the year included Barbie, Bratz, Cars: The Movie, Crayola, and Dora the Explorer, with properties such as Air Hogs, Hannah Montana, Spider-Man, Transformers, and Webkinz experiencing the most growth. Licensed toys represented

27 percent of total industry sales in 2007, with Cars: The Movie, Disney Princess, Dora the Explorer, Spider-Man, and Star Wars leading the list of best-selling licensed toys.

According to NPD, an emerging trend in the industry is the increase in sales of connected Web play toys.

"Connected Web play toys, which marry a physical toy with ongoing digital play opportunities via the Internet, is a relatively new phenomenon that we've seen emerge within the toy industry," said Anita Frazier analyst, The NPD Group. "Thanks in large part to the popular "Thanks in large part to the popular Webkinz brand, this type of play is expanding into new categories and across many properties" (Tekrati 2008).

For the movie season of 2005-06 was "Star Wars III: Revenge of the Sith,"the series from which Darth Vader hails.

Lucasfilm reports a $9 billion sales figure for Star Wars franchise merchandise, proving the insatiable demand for Star Wars tie-in products. 4/29/2005 (Price: $14.99; Age: 3 and Up) (Abrahams, 2005, p.1).

The recent hype and success of Harry Potter, as well as other children's characters has led to further sales for toy manufacturers. But as well as perhaps bringing joy and fun to children, as a report from U.S.-based National Labor Committee says, for workers who have to make these toys, these can be "Toys of Misery". Quoted from that report here at length, is part of the preface:

"When you go into a Wal-Mart or a Toys 'R' Us store to purchase Harry Potter or Disney's Monsters Inc., Mattel's Barbie, Sesame Street, Hasbro's Star Wars or Pokemon do you ever think of the young women in China forced to work 16 hours a day, from 8:00 a.m. to 12 midnight, seven days a week, 30 days a month, for months on end, for wages of 17 cents an hour? Workers forced to work overtime, but cheated of their pay? Do you ever imagine women working all day long in 104-degree temperatures, handling toxic glues, paints and solvents, women fainting, nauseous, sick to their stomachs? Women housed 16 to a dorm room and trying to get by on four hours of sleep a night? Workers whose bodies ache, who are exhausted from racing through the same operations 3,000 times a day, day in and day out? Women who are fired when they get sick? Workers who have no rights, and who–if they try to defend their most basic, internationally recognized human and worker rights will be immediately fired and blacklisted? Workers who are worn out and used up by the time they reach 30 or 35 years of age and are removed to be replaces with another crop of young teenagers? Unfortunately, this is the real world behind the toys we purchase in the United States. And we do purchase a staggering number of toys each year: 3.6 billion toys in the year 2000 alone–76 million dolls, 349 million plush toys, 125 million action figures, 279 million hot wheels and matchbox cars, 88 million sporting goods items and so on. This is big industry. **We spend more than $29.4 billion a year on toys.**

According to The Montreal Gazette (2008) in Quebec Canada the toy safety standards rose even though Health Canada had still not approved lead testing for toys in 2008.

Option consommateurs tested 300 toys for quality, playability, safety and overall value, including 252 new toys. Organizers said there are a number of good toys on the market this year. Of the 252 new toys, 186 were deemed 'recommended' or 'very good' (Naud 2008, pp.5-7).

Among this year's top toys:

- Mont-a-Mots Pictos, a memory and association game by Lampiste, $25, 31/2 to 7 years
- A make-it yourself colouring kit by Djeco, $25, 7 to 10 years
- Six, a strategy game from Fox Mind Games, $20, 7 and up

Among this year's worst toys:

- The Kiddieland Light 'n Sound Turtle, $22, 11/2 to 21/2years
- Crayola Beginnings Creativity Central, $22, 2 to 4 years
- KidKleen Mold 'n Play Soap, $6, 3 to 6 years
- Crayola Model Magic Fusion, $10, 6 to 8 years
- Kid Galaxy Bump 'n Chuck remote-control Bumper Cars, $35, 6 to 10 years (Gazette, 2008, p.7).

Eighty percent of all the toys we purchase are imports, and 71 percent of those are from China. **More than one out of every two toys we purchase in the U.S. is made in China.** We purchase hundreds of millions of toys each year that are made in China, but when was the last time we heard from a toy worker in China about their working conditions and lives? Even once? Ever? Isn't it a little strange that we know so little?

In 2000, U.S. toy companies spent $837 million on advertising. The companies do not want us to know or to think, just to buy (Toys of Misery Report, 2001).

Hughes (2005) clearly points out that Age compression, the idea that kids are getting older younger, is a term used often among toy manufacturers, retailers and other industry insiders. The reality of age compression can be seen when looking at the downturn in sales of traditional toys like action figures. While 2004 was a fairly flat year for action figure sales, the previous year saw an 18 percent drop in goods sold.

"Kids are growing up earlier and they're abandoning traditional toys for products that are not generated or even traditionally marketed to them, like video games, iPods and cell phones," says David Riley of The NPD Group. Electronic items–traditionally adult "toys" are becoming the top entry on every child's wish list, and action figure sales are suffering as a consequence.

According to Steve, the manager of Toys 'R Us in Fort Wayne, Ind., whose last name had to be withheld because of company policy, his store carries less of an assortment of figures than it did in the past. "It really began about four years ago," the manager said. "There is more of an interest in electronics, like **Game Boy** and **Play Station.** "Action figures are real popular with collectors, but sales die off after Christmas, and they're even down during Christmas from what they were a few years ago."

GameBoy

Yet says Datamonitor (2006):

> Whether used for fun or learning, young kids' toys are their tools. As of 2005, the ITP toy industry has built sales to $4.5 billion, by providing the coolest and most efficient tools possible, utilizing licenses (from Dora the Explorer to Winnie the Pooh), educational features, and as always, ingenious design: Such factors are bigger drivers than the slowly growing ITP population." (p.1).

Another example related both to children as well as the more general culture and media, is that of Disney, as mentioned on this web site's media ownership section.

"No one's really worrying about what it's [advertising to children] is teaching impressionable youth. Hey, I'm in the business of convincing people to buy things they don't need" –an advertising executive, in Business Week, August 11, 1997, quoted by Richard Robbins

8. Active children are healthy children generally speaking

GAMES–Create your own games; yes, you CAN!

To comment on the marketing of toys based on adult entertainment, such as mature or adult-rated movies or video games:

If the advertisement is on television, contact the TV station in question.

You should also send your comments to Advertising Standards Canada (ASC), the Canadian Radio-television and Telecommunications Commission (CRTC) and the Canadian Broadcast Standards Council (CBSC), using the complaint forms on their Web sites.

If the advertisement is in a magazine, contact the magazine or newspaper in question and the company that owns the publication. For Canadian publications, you should also contact Advertising Standards Canada (ASC), using the complaints form on their Web site.

As well, check your local toy store to see if it sells children's toys that are based on adult entertainment. Send a letter to the store manager, and your local newspaper, outlining your concerns.

Here are some other issues to think of.

9. Create your labels. What will they look like and stand for?

10. Counterfeits and high school exploits with greed and gambling. –addictions, addictions, addictions! Students tried in 2004 to print their own money in one area high school. Ooh la lah, no, no! NO LICENCE TO PRINT MONEY Image and Substance- Sleight-of-hand? Are there other ways to get around a cash economy? Could you trade services, time, favours, or goods with others?

The BBC, reporting on this (April 29, 2003), commented the following, amongst other things:

> One set of posts and nets for volleyball would require tokens from 5,440 bars of chocolate. This would require spending £2,000 (about $3,500) on chocolate and wolfing their way through 1.25 million calories, some 2 million kilos of fat. A basketball would be 170 bars of chocolate, which, if it were to be burned off, a 10-year-old child would need to play for 90 hours. While the confectionary companies suggest that children are going to eat these anyway, others raise concerns that this is promoting unhealthier eating. The chairman of the UK government's obesity taskforce, Professor Phil James, said: "This is a classic example of how the food and soft drink industry are failing to take on board that they are major contributors to obesity problems throughout the world. They always try to divert attention to physical activity."

What is more, as most British media outlets also highlighted, was that this was with the thumbs up from the government because the minister for sport Richard Caborn endorsed it.

11. Valuing our Human Qualities
What Values could you prioritze as the most important 5 in your family life?

12. Advocating better Labour Conditions in the "Poor" Countries.

Open Secrets about Labour Outsourcing

Diddy Did

And finally, last year at this time I wrote you about Sean Combs (a.k.a. P. Diddy). Well, I'm glad to report that Sean Combs did the right thing. Today, at the SETISA factory in Honduras, mandatory pregnancy tests have ended; the worst supervisors have been fired, so the women are no longer hit and abused; there is clean drinking water; the locks have been taken off the bathrooms; the factory is air-conditioned; the workers have health insurance; overtime is voluntary and correctly paid, and the workers have a union! Solidarity works! But I would be being dishonest with you if I said that the anti-sweatshop movement were in great shape.

If the American retailers paid only 25 cents more per garment, the total in Bangladesh would be $898 million–more than eight times current US aid. 21 Dec 2004.

End the Superexploitation by:

13. Raising Awareness of Social Budgeting.

14. Remembering the world before the Internet and linking arms in the Village.

15. Unmasking Nihilism, Denial, and Lies in Denying Human Authenticity.

16. Exposing Discrimination in Health Services-Our Bodies Ourselves.

17. Combating Discrimination in Advertising.

After all, looking back in time a mite, wouldn't every young athlete like to be able to jump like Dr. J? Wouldn't every prospective NFL lineman or overweight ex-jock like to be as strong as Bubba Smith? And wouldn't everyone like to pig out and get paid for it like The Refrigerator? Of course, minorities also appear prominently in all kinds of ads in minority media. That's known as market segmentation. If you are aiming for Ebony or Essence readers, use famous blacks or at least black models. If you want to reach Spanish International Network TV viewers, use Latinos. And the beat goes on. Maybe I'm overstating the case. Or maybe I'm just a 1960s dinosaur, victimized by too much hope for integration. Change comes slowly everywhere, including in advertising. But it's certainly time to hope and work for a faster pace (Datamonitor, 2006).

18. Tobacco and alcohol

"Advertising has always sold anxiety, and it certainly sells anxiety to the young. It's always telling them they're losers unless they're cool (Miller, 2000)."

Tobacco and alcohol companies have long targeted young people, hoping to develop brand loyalties that will last a lifetime.

It's crucial for the tobacco industry to continually cultivate new and younger smokers to replace the thousands who quit each year—and those who die of tobacco-related diseases.

The tobacco industry targets youth by: linking smoking in ads with being "cool" and independent and with taking risks (particularly physical risks) placing ads in magazines with high adolescent readerships, such as Rolling Stone, Maxim or People having movie stars, who are popular with young people, smoke in films sponsoring rock concerts and sporting events placing advertising near high schools: on billboards, in bus shelters and in variety stores.

The alcohol and beer industries were quick to recognize the value of the Internet as an effective tool for reaching young people. The Web offers marketers a medium that is a huge part of youth culture—with the added bonus that it's unregulated, with very little parental supervision.

In 1999, the U.S. Center for Media Education found that 62 per cent of beer and alcohol Web sites displayed what they call "youth-oriented features"—that is, activities that appeal to the adolescent and pre-adolescent set.

The alcohol and beer industries also target youth by: running ads during TV shows with a high number of young views, such as The Simpsons, South Park or sporting events placing ads in magazines with high adolescent readerships, such as Rolling Stone, Maxim or People sponsoring rock concerts and sporting events creating and extensively marketing "alcopops"—sweetened, lightly carbonated drinks that don't taste like alcohol (think Mike's Hard Lemonade) (Media-awareness 2005).

THE MAIN IDEA IS CRYSTAL CLEAR HERE–BUY, BUY, BUY! (for a different meaning of a healthful variety of COOL, look around you and observe what is acceptable as 'cool' today.

Tape some of the Teens' definitions of what "COOL" means to them).

19 Protest, Demonstration, Letters, and Petitions to the Fore

Research and try to comprehend the background of some sample letters and adapt to your purposes.

Studies have also found that boys, like girls, may turn to smoking to help them lose weight.

Other topics to explore:

20. Sports Heroes on Steroids and Other Substances

21. Impossible Chocolate Wrapper Contests are like asking the Rest of the World to Stop Begging So Hard–Land of Woe-Mart and Money

22. Place of Art, Religion, Music, and in Things in Life

The public fetishistically substitutes consumer ideals for the lost acculturating experiences of art, religion and family. The consumer sublimates the desire for cultural fulfillment to the rewards of buying and owning commodities, and substitutes media-manipulated undulations in the public persona for spiritual rebirth. In the myth of consumerism, there is no rebirth or renewal. And there are no iconic symbols to evoke transcendent truths. ©R. Cronk 1996 - All Rights Reserved

Suggested Research Topics for a 1 page Report:

23. Natural Highs and Ego Satisfaction

24. Moral Lows and Media

25. Open-mindedness

26. Freeing learning canons, cultures, and academic icons e.g. SATS

27. The Hallowed Dollar

28. Enter Darth Vader and the Establishment of Evil Empires

Big Business as the Enemy of the People

Tens of thousands of teenage women in Bangladesh sewing clothing for Wal-Mart clean their teeth each morning using a finger and ashes from the fire, since they cannot afford a toothbrush, which costs 25 cents, or toothpaste, which costs 51 cents. They earn just 13 cents an hour. It is common for eight workers to share one room, with five people sleeping on a wooden platform and three on the ground. The roof leaks when it rains, so the women have to sit up at night covering themselves with pieces of plastic.

In China, women assembling toys for Wal-Mart smuggled their time cards out of the factory. Incredibly, they were working 130 hours a week with shifts stretching from 7:51 a.m. straight through to 4:31 a.m. the following day. They earned 16 ½ cents per hour. Wal-Mart's profits last year-made off the backs of exploited young women across the developing world were $9.1 billion, and the Walton family alone is worth $90 billion.

Consumer Ideals

According to Professor Juliet Schor: (2003) and I quote her at length for she is so tuned into our contemporary corporate consumer pulse: By the time many children reach early elementary school, they have already been incorporated into the universe of junk entertainment, listening to music and watching movies and television that offer them unprecedented levels of violence along with the presentation of young people as sexual objects. (MTV isn't just for teenagers, it's a kid phenomenon, too.) By the time these kids enter the 8 to 12 "tween" stage, they've adopted the junk values of materialism and the desire to be rich. When I interviewed Martin Lindstrom, a branding expert, he cited a recent survey by the Millward Brown global market research agency. It reveals that nowhere else in the world are 8- to 12-year-olds more materialistic (75 percent desire to be "rich,") or more likely to believe that their clothes and brands describe who they are and define their social status.

All this is not only distasteful, it is unhealthy, as I found after surveying 300 children ages 10 to 13 in urban and suburban Boston in 2002 and 2003. Perhaps, as they focus on the consumer culture, kids spend less time in the reading and play that keeps them happy and healthy. Difficult as it is to explain, the connection is clear: The more enmeshed children are in the culture of getting and spending, the more they suffer for it. purveyors and reclaimed the culture of childhood. (Author's e-mail: /schorj@bc.edu <mailto:schorj@bc.edu/Juliet Schor is a professor of sociology at Boston College and the author of a new book, "Born to Buy: The Commercialized Child and the New Consumer Culture" (Scribner). She is on the advisory board of Commercial.

The Credit Seduction and The Debt Trap

March 12th, 2003-Forty-six (46%) percent of Americans are making minimum or no payments on their credit card balances, according to the Cambridge Consumer Credit Index. Amount Canadians owed on their Visa and MasterCards by the end of 2003: $49.8 billion. Percentage of Canadian Visa/MasterCard holders who haven't paid their bill in three months or more in 2003: 0.8% (CBC, 2003).

Cooperatives and Credit Unions as a Means to End Poverty

The Nobel Prize awarded to Dr. Muhammad Yunus of Bangladesh in 2006 points the way too how microcredit can be help to women, men, and children wishing to fulfill their economic goals. This is similar to the use that credit has traditionally been put in credit unions to helping people succeed with their businesses and personal financial needs. Cooperative ownership of business has been another way to get around finding money to help build and sustain community business.

History of Credit Unions

Credit unions are a financial cooperative. They are member owned, democratically run and have a volunteer board chosen from the membership, by the membership.

Hermann Schulze-Delitzsch put forth effort for credit unions in order to help combat poverty and created a credit union in Germany in 1852. Friedrich Wilhelm Raiffeisen is remembered as the father of the credit union movement. In 1864 as Mayor of Flammersfeld, Germany, he asked his people to pool their savings and make loans to one another at reasonable rates. The principles he used to establish the credit union are still fundamental today.

He went on to start more than 425 credit unions.

Alphonse Desjardins, a Canadian journalist, brought the idea of credit unions to North America. In 1901 he opened the first North American credit union in Quebec, Canada.

Not long after, Edward Filene, a wealthy department store owner heard about credit unions and was convinced they would help people. Pierre Jay, a bank commissioner in Massachusetts, reached the same conclusion. He and Filene met with Desjardins, who helped them start the first credit union (St. Mary's Bank) in the United States, namely, Manchester, New Hampshire.

Filene hired a lawyer by the name of Roy F. Bergensen. By 1921, they had started a national organization to promote credit unions. In 1934 this organization became known as the Credit Union National Association (CUNA) focusing on serving credit unions and has continued to do this important job.

In 1934, the Federal Credit Union Act, a federal law allowing credit unions to be incorporated in any state in the country, was signed by President Franklin D. Roosevelt.

History of Cooperatives

Cooperatives are businesses, in many ways like any other business. But a cooperative belongs to the people who use it, and it operates solely for the members' benefit. Cooperatives vary, but all co-op businesses run in accordance with seven basic principles, many of which have been part of the co-op philosophy from their beginnings more than 150 years ago.

1. Open and voluntary membership. It's important that members choose voluntarily to become members. Coerced membership would be meaningless.
2. Democratic member control. Members ultimately control their cooperatives, in a democratic manner.

3. Member economic participation. "Cooperatives operate so that capital is the servant, not the master, of the organization."
4. Autonomy and independence. While governments determine the legislative framework within which co-ops function, this principle asserts that co-ops also have an "essential need to be autonomous in the same way that enterprises controlled by capital are…"
5. Education, training, and information. This principle says members can play their role in the cooperative only when they understand that role and the co-op.
6. Cooperation among cooperatives. Cooperators believe that co-ops have a unique opportunity to protect and expand the interest of ordinary people. This kind of one-for-all and all-for-one idea is unique among businesses.
7. Concern for community. Cooperatives exist primarily for the benefit of their members. Because of this strong association with members, they also are often closely and actively tied to their communities.

Ben Franklin helped establish the first co-op in Philadelphia in 1752. In 1844 a poverty stricken area organized a cooperative in Rochdale, England. That same year, cooperative theories were developed. Credit societies were a part of that effort.

References

Abraham, K. (2005). TDmonthly's Top 10 Most Wanted Action Figure. Retrieved January 24, 2005 from http://www.toydirectory.com/monthly/article.asp?id=1336

Badoe http://www.google.com/imgres?imgurl=http://www.umanitoba.ca/outreach/cm/vol8/no14/thepotofwisdom.jpg&imgrefurl=http://www.umanitoba.ca/cm/vol8/no14/ananse.html&h=255&w=202&sz=19&tbnid=t3H3TcZ58hgJ::&tbnh=111&tbnw=88&prev=/images%3Fq%3Dimages%2Bof%2Blegendary%2Bcharacter%2Bin%2Bafrican%2Bfolklore&hl=en&usg=__xFLf2TlRNrg-PXiGwSNfyOLGmaQ=&sa=X&oi=image_result&resnum=2&ct=image&cd=1 Retrieved June 12, 2008

Datamonitor. (2006). Age Compression Challenges Action Figure . Retrieved January 24, 2006 from http://www.mindbranch.com/products/R567-502.html

Hughes, T. (2005). Age Compression Challenges Action Figure . Retrieved January 24, 2006 from http://www.toydirectory.com/monthly/article.asp?id=1306

Miller, M. (2000). The Merchants of Cool. Retrieved October 11, 2005 from http://www.pbs.org/cgi-registry/stationlink.cgir

POTTER Jonathan Henderson By Amy Jussel, October 10, 2006 p.1 http://www.commonsenseblog.org/archives/2006/10/were_barely_bac.php pp.1-2.

Christine http://64.233.169.104/search?q=cache:bMt_FCJHjW4J:www2.ville.montreal.qc.ca/jardin/premieres_nations/program/programmation_2008.pdf+winoosis+and+Christine+Sioui+Wawanoloath,+artist+and+author+Abenaki-Wendat&hl=en&ct=clnk&cd=1&gl=ca&lr=lang_fr&client=firefox-a

Rachel Naud , For Neighbours http://www.canada.com/topics/lifestyle/parenting/story.html?id=9aee3282-2642-4b15-a482-d7a23bc0d529 Retrieved November 7, 2008, pp.1-2 **The Calgary Herald** 2008

Toys of Misery; A Report on the Toy Industry in China, National Labor Committee, December 2001.

Yunus, M. (2006). Dr. Muhammad Yunus: 2006 Nobel Peace Prize Laureate. Retrieved April 19, 2007 from http://www.muhammadyunus.org/

Awareness and Education for Consumerist Understanding, Reflection, and Action

Get active! Organize an anti-consumerism event in your school or community. Host a Violent Toy Turn-In event at your school, church or community centre:

Invite families in your community to turn in their violent toys, such as action figures, guns and other weapons. If you hold your event during the Christmas shopping season you can make it into a toy fair and invite neighbourhood toy stores to set up displays of non-violent toys and books.

Enlist the help of a local artist to create a sculpture from the toys that are turned in. Make sure to invite the media to cover your event. Try to figure out 10 Steps for Planning a Successful Violent Toy Turn-In Day handout.

Finding Voice as a Person

Here are some more ways to express your thoughts and feelings through acts that empower you to achieve your goals.

VOICE FOUND FOR ACTION!

In addition to the list below kindly add your Action List:

1. --

----

2. --

----

3. --

----

4. --

----

5. --

----

6. --

----

7. --

8.--

----

9. --

----

10. --

More Ideas

Advertising Positive Human Values vs. Consumerism

1. Have fun creating your "commercials" for: radio, television, internet, movies, and anti-bias in advertising.

Also: **Taking Action**

It's important that consumers voice their opinions about advertising to the industry.

To comment on a print advertisement:
- Contact the magazine or newspaper in question and the company that owns the publication.
- For Canadian publications, you should also contact Advertising Standards Canada (ASC), using the complaints form on their Web site. If you send a letter, you should enclose a copy of the offending advertisement.

To comment on a commercial on TV or radio:
- Contact the TV or radio station in question.
- You should also send your comments to Advertising Standards Canada (ASC), the Canadian Radio-television and Telecommunications Commission (CRTC) and the Canadian Broadcast Standards Council (CBSC), using the complaint forms on their Web sites.

You should have the following information when making a complaint about an ad on TV or radio: the station on which it was aired; the date and approximate time it aired; the name of the product; and why you think the advertisement contravenes Canadian advertising codes. For information on the codes see the Understanding Advertising Guidelines and Codes section.

To comment on advertisements for adult or teen-rated movies shown during children's movies or TV:

- If the advertisement is shown at a theatre during a movie meant for a younger audience, complain to the theatre management.
- If the ad is shown on TV during programming meant for young children, you should contact the TV station in question. You should also send your comments to Advertising Standards Canada (ASC), the Canadian Radio-television and Telecommunications Commission (CRTC) and the Canadian Broadcast Standards Council (CBSC), using the complaint forms on their Web sites.

To comment on commercials in movie theatres:

- If you object to sitting through a string of commercials in a theatre before the feature film starts, you can lodge a complaint with the theatre management.
- Don't forget about positive feedback!
- Marketers need to be complimented when they produce socially responsible, positive advertisements. The MediaWatch and About-Face Web sites feature examples of advertisements that promote positive images of women and children.

2. Celebrate Buy Nothing Day with your school or Guide/Scout unit:

- The idea behind this international event is to encourage consumers to examine their spending habits, and to think about the effect of mass consumerism on the cultural and natural environment of the world.

- Contact your local media and ask them to cover your activities. For more information, see (Buy Nothing Day, 2005). Stop commercialization in your school or school district.
- Work with your school's parent and student councils and your school trustees to develop guidelines for commercialization in your school or district.
- Make sure your local media is aware of your efforts. For more information: (see the Make Your School Commercial Free Zone, 2005). Educate parents in your school community: Organize a parent media awareness group at your school. You can gauge the level of interest (and clarify your priorities and goals) by sending a copy of the Your Family and Media survey (2005).
- Awareness raising and Unbranding the Fruits of Labour

3. Encouraging Childrens' Successes in Schools

4. Turn Around the Symbols of Celebrity Status with Unifying Thoughts and Acts

5. Decisions, Decisions–Do Something for Heaven's Sake!

6. Media Obsessions and Balance

7. Parents as Agents of Childrens' Education

Taking Action
Read article below [Appendix in Chapter 4 Is Anyone to Blame for the American Drop-out Rate? (Reyner, 2003) and RECOGNIZING AND MEDIATING:

8. Alienation and Attendant Social, Criminal, or Deviant Behaviours

9. Keeping the public in School Funding

10. Making Schools Friendlier to Change

11. Segregation as an Ongoing Problem in Schools (use anti-bias programs in folders)

Life is Not a Commodity
Topic: Water

Anita Roddick (2005) warned:
Britain's development aid is being siphoned off for big business. Find out how taxpayers money is funding the corporate takeover of the world's water and hear from grassroots campaigners who are fighting back. The World Development Movement is hosting a series of talks by Ghanaian activists who are resisting the privatisation of their country's water supply.

Water is as essential to us as making sure that we survive as a planet and those living and non-living things that inhabit it. We might also make comparisons between the survival issues of say water, renewable energy sources, health challenges like AIDS/HIV in European or North American lifestyles with the battle to survive in Africa. In South Africa, for example, we could look briefly at one such organization that tries to make life better for children.

The Thandanani Foundation.

Thandanani Childrens FoundationThandanani means "Love One Another" and the organisation aims to bring hope to the lives of children. Thandanani Childrens Foundation is a registered non-profit organisation constituted as a Section 21 Company (Thandanani, 2004).

Thandanani is aware of the issues facing the children of South Africa, in particular those in the Pietermaritzburg area of KwaZulu-Natal. We are committed to ensuring these issues are addressed by empowering the communities that the children are based in to deals with the issues in a positive and constructive manner. There are many different aspects of our work, from establishing a presence in the community so that childrens' issues are highlighted and dealt with at this level to creating an awareness in government of the impracticalities of the social welfare system (e.g. 49% of children don't have identification documents, but these are a requirement for accessing social grants!) and our website attempts to provide some insight into our operation and success!

Below are some of the issues that we are trying to deal with:

KEY ISSUES FACING CHILDREN
Poverty & Social Welfare

- 12.3 million children, between 0 and 18 years, live in poverty in South Africa
- Only limited social welfare support is available and access is difficult
- The unemployment rate for KwaZulu-Natal is estimated at 37%
- The communities in Pietermaritzburg and surrounding areas, served by Thandanani Childrens Foundation are

characterised by pervasive poverty.
- Impact of HIV/AIDS. The national HIV & Syphilis Sero. Prevalence rates are as follows:
  - In 2001:24.8% of women visiting antenatal clinics were infected
  - 4.74 million people were infected
  - 25% of children in State Hospitals are HIV+
  - By 2010, it is estimated that there will be 2.5 million orphans as a result of HIV/Aids with 900,000 Child Headed Households
- It is estimated that by 2010 KwaZulu-Natal will have 500,000 Orphans and Pietermaritzburg will have 50,000

Vulnerability of Children

Within this context, children are extremely vulnerable in terms of:
- Hunger
- A lack of shelter, security of tenure and physical protection
- Access to educational opportunities
- The increasing number of child-headed households-The need to care for dying parents
- Exposure to violence and sexual abuse
- Teenage pregnancy
- Child labour
- Lack of access to play and recreation
- Lack of emotional and developmental support.

End Activity:

Survey (answer the following questions):

Who is your (a) hero (b) a political figure (c) an activist (d) a family member or friend (e) a celebrity (f) a teacher, or (g) a spiritual person?

References

Bracey, G. (2002). The war against America's public schools: Privatizing schools, commercializing education. Boston: Allyn & Bacon.

Buy Nothing Day: Activities for the Classroom and Home. (2004). Retrieved 25 March, 2005 from
http://www.media-awareness.ca/english/resources/educational/teaching_backgrounders/advertising_marketing/buy_nothing_day.cfm

CBC (2003). Home: CBC.ca http://www.cbc.ca/CBC Radio Retrieved January 5, 2005 from http://www.cbc.ca/programguide/radio/>CBC Television).

Cook, D. (2001). Lunchbox hegemony; Kids and the Marketplace, Then & Now. LiP Magazine (on line), Aug. 20. Retrieved November 4, 2005 from http://www.lipmagazine.org.

Cortes, C. (2000) The Children Are Watching: how the media teach about diversity. New York: Teachers College Press.

Huffman, T. (2001). Resistance theory and the transculturation hypothesis as explanations of college attrition and persistence among culturally traditional American Indian students. Journal of American Indian Education, 40, 3, pp.1-23.

Making Your School a Commercial-Free Zone. Retrieved 25 March, 2005 from http://www.media awareness.ca/english/resources/tip_sheets/school_commercial_tip.cfm 25-03-05) tip sheet.

McChesney, R. (2000). The Merchants of Cool. Retrieved October 11, 2005 from http://www.pbs.org/cgi-registry/stationlink.cgir

McPherson, W. (1984). Testing The Current. New York: Simon & Schuster.

Ogbu, J. (2003). Black American students in an affluent suburb: A study of academic disengagement. Mawah, NJ: Lawrence Erlbaum.

Reyhner, J. (2003). Is Anyone to Blame for the American Drop-out Rate? Indigenous Education , NABE News Columns 2000 Volume 26, No.6, pp. 26-27, July/August 2003 ???? Northern Arizona University

Reyhner, J. (1992a). Plans for dropout prevention and special school support services for American Indian and Alaska Native students. Retrieved June 9, 2003 from http://jan.ucc.nau.edu/~jar/INAR.html

Reyhner, J. (1992). American Indians out of school: A review of school-based causes and solutions. Journal of American Indian Education, 31, 3, pp.37-56. Retrieved June 9, 2003 from http://jaie.asu.edu/v31/V31S3ind.htm

Roddick, A (2005). Life is Not a Commodity. Retrieved date April 4, 2005 from http://www.anitaroddick.com/topicdetails.php?topicid=47&PHPSESSID=9db1dbfaa0489f3bb70330f42d3fb81c

Schor, J. (2003). The Stepford Kids Born To Buy: The Commercialized Child and the New Consumer Culture. New York: Scribner.

Thandanani Childrens Foundation. (2004).Thandanani © Copyright According to International Copyright Laws

Toys of Misery; A Report on the Toy Industry in China. (2000). National Labor Committee, December.

Working to End Sweatshops Working to End Sweatshops. (1995). Retrieved May 26, 2005 from https://www.paypal.com/xclick/business=ssarkar%40nlcnet.org&item_name=+%26+Child+Labor&no_shipping=1&return=http%3A//www.nlcnet.org/thanks.shtml&no_note=1&tax=0&currency_code=USD (pp.38-39 op cit)

Your Family and Media survey. (2005). Retrieved 25 March, 2005 from http://www.media awareness.ca/english/resources/parents_resources/handouts/handouts_family_survey.cfm home to parents with your school newsletter

More Ideas, Activities, Brainwaves to Spark Family Involvements in Healthy Growth

1. **Nature Appreciation**
    *   Build a Diorama of Dolphins at Play
    *   Make a large plastic Dolphin and Paint it in your own colour schema
    *   Research, organize, and Go Swimming with Dolphins
    *   Create a pair of Dolphin Earrings
    *   Fund raise to adopt a Dolphin

2. Laughter
+ Write a 2 page Comedy Skit
+ Act out the above Skit
+ Design Posters to advertise your Skit
+ Make an iPod Movie of your Skit
+ Build a Laugh Meter to test different Audiences Laughter Volumes

---

3. Entrepreneurship for the Well being of All
+ Projects to eliminate world hunger
+ Healthcare Fundraisers
+ Human Rights Advocacy for Children
+ Ecology and Environment Protection

---

4. Homemade Toys for Children
+ Pete's Robot (drawing)
+ Make a Giant Robot (8 feet tall)
+ Make a Recipe for a New Type of Chocolate Bar
+ Write a Nursery Rhyme
+ Fashion a Wooden Miniature Applecart that reflects a Wild Theme
+ Put a Tall Tale on Tape

---

5. Insects that Fascinate Me
+ Tish's Butterfly (imagine and draw)

- Draw a Caterpillar (14x8 inches)
- Pattern A Story Board about "A Termite-on-the-Road" (Make a Blueprint)
- Make up a Song about the Cricket in the Hedge
- Collect Larvae and Frame it in Kaleidoscope

---

6. Phips' "Deep Blue" (Radio) (Drawing)

- Invention
- Make a Sound Byte of Your Choral or Music Group
- A Mechanical Helper around the House
- A Service for a dis/abled Person in your Neighbourhood
- Monitor your Favourite Shortwave Station and Keep a Log (5 quick points on each show for a month and then write to the show's producers sharing your feelings and thoughts about that Show)
- Mix a Music Tape/ A Multimedia CD/DVD selected from Sounds in Nature

---

7. Games that Entertain

- Work out a Plan for the following Game Boards and go on to Finalize a Laminated Copy (28x 11 inches of larger)
- Shakes and Doodles
- Broccoli Pie

- Formula Car Racing
- Winner Takes All
- Alpha's mask

---

8. Using My Positive Qualities- for example, My (-: Smile. Fill in the blanks below and go for it!

---

9. Honesty in Media Advertising

- Interview a friend who Uses Your Product (cereal, videogame, book etc.)
- Write a Letter to the Media stating a Point of View (TV, Radio, Internet, Cellphone)
- Radio Station for Kids
- Produce a TV Show for an After School Homework and Tutoring Program
- Create a Hot Air Balloon for Your Message of Peace in the Universe(s)

---

10. Substance Abuse

- Make Terrarium in a Bottle
- Re-design a Clean Air Carton with A Good Health Message
- Pull together a Concert for a Worthy Cause
- Mix a New Fruit Punch
- Keep a Journal on Insecurities You face on a Daily Basis

11. Fair Trade

+ Coffee Fair
+ Chocolate Party
+ Gold Earrring Display
+ Sugar Cookie Cutters
+ Rice Pudding for Freedom

---

12. High Finance

+ The Money Game
+ Invent a Solar Technological Gadget to help Women Cook Food
+ Set up a Neighbourhood Bank to Fund Worthy Projects in Your Community
+ Make Miming Game with Truth or Dare as a Theme to Help Entrepreneurs Move Ahead with Their Projects
+ Design a Database to List Urgent Needs in your Community

---

13. Elders and Children

+ Tell A Story to Children about Your Youth
+ Record on Cassette Tape a Tale told by an Elder
+ Compile a Photo Album of "An Elder Journey"
+ Organize a Sing-a-long for Children and Elders
+ Videogames and Elders' Projects

14. The Power of One to Change Life
- A Rescue Squad to Help Others
- Write a Plan to Help Improve a Government Service
- Involve a Pro BonoLawyer to Help a Cause of Your Choice
- Get Help from a Volunteer Nurse to Help a Teen In Need
- Get a Doctor to Speak to your Group about AIDS/HIV

15. Entertainment Night
- Variety Time for All Ages:
- Comics
- Clowns
- Puppets
- Satirists
- Jugglers

16. Sports and Fun
- Indoor Tournament Weekend:
- Soccer
- Baseball
- Hockey
- Football
- Track

17. Lighthearted Get-Togethers

+ Popcorn Balls
+ Name Games
+ Spontaneous 1 minute speeches (topics drawn from hat)
+ Quick Drawing on a Silly Theme
+ Running-On-The-Spot Marathon for World Poverty Elimination
+ Joke a thon

18. Learning a New Skill

+ Darts
+ Rings
+ Bagatelle
+ Chess
+ Bridge

19. Arts and Crafts Collage-Making

+ Leather pouch
+ Embroidered Mandala
+ Sand Art
+ Metal Belt Clasp
+ Woollen Hat

20. Natural Highs for Ego Taming

+ Quiet Reflection (10 mins.)
+ Giving an Hour of Your Time to Help Out
+ Literacy Tutoring
+ Making a Sports' Recreation Club
+ Live Acoustic Music Jamboree

---

21. Sailing Through Bad News Media

+ Finding Positive Qualities in Difficult Situations Observation Activities
+ Constructive Anti-Poverty Projects
+ Sponsored Reading Contests
+ Everyone–Wins Soccer Challenge Games
+ Talking to Business and Government Leaders about Raising the Bar on Honesty

---

21. Openmindedness

+ Learn and Practise a New Attitude Towards Someone You Hold a Bias against because of by (a) Developing an Imaginary Conversational Dialogue between the two of you and (b) Acting on your new attitude:
+ Culture
+ Dis/Abilty
+ Race and Physical Characteristics
+ Religion
+ Dress
+ Speech

21. Symbols

* Totem-making to Show One World One Love for People
* Pottery Bowls and Dishes for Hungry People
* Masks to Help Express Emotions
* Iron Sculpture From Used Metals To Joy
* Imagined Time Capsules of History

---

22. The Hallowed and Respectfulness

* Fasting
* Kneeling
* Prayer
* Touch
* Walking
* 23. Fairness
* Work
* Sport
* Children
* Women
* Men

---

23. Community Business

* Co-operatives
* Guilds
* Clubs
* Savings Banks
* Barter Points

24. Consumer Ideals
+ Letter to Ralph Nader
+ Videogame Designs for Peace
+ Born-to-Share Posters
+ Parents' Bill of Rights
+ Good Behaviour-in-School Awards Certificates

25. Re-popularizing Pop Music
+ Biographies
+ Timelines
+ Songs
+ Favourite Star's recipes
+ Diaries

26. Finding Our Voices
+ Choral Song
+ Pantomime
+ Marathons
+ Hospital Visits
+ Museums

27. Human Values Messages for:
+ Internet
+ Radio
+ Television

* Movies
* Advertising

---

28. Celebrate Buy-Nothing-Day

* Work With Your School to Create a Buy-Nothing Agenda
* Plan School Activities
* Contact the Local Media to Publicize Events
* Carry Out Activities
* Celebrate Success with Home Baking Party

---

29. Improving Schools

* Finding ways to Welcome Newcomers Cordially
* Forming Meaningful Study Groups
* Teacher-Student Recreation
* Diversity Appreciation Contact Meetings/Socials
* Projects to Advance Unity in Diversity

---

30. Boosting Your Parents' Can-Do Attitudes

* Honouring Parents Actions
* Honing in on Parents Skills for School
* Computer Games with Student and parent (not your own)
* Celebrity for School Support
* Parents Stories of Adversity and Triumph

31. Prevent Deforestation
+ Plant a Tree
+ Advocate for More Green Space Preservation
+ Exchange Tree Seeds with Penpals Overseas
+ River Beds Diving Course
+ Save Timber from River Beds

32. Respecting Immigration
+ No Illegal Residents
+ Buddy Linking
+ Listening to "Their"/story
+ Teach One
+ Feed One
+ Help One

33. Pets
+ Prevention of Cruelty
+ Loving
+ Making Healthy Homemade Pet Foods
+ Freeing Birds
+ Camera Hunting

34. Food
+ Open Dating of Foods
+ List of Food Ingredients with Calories Contents

+ No Dumping of Excess Food
+ Feeding the Hungry People of the World
+ Cookouts, BBQs, Multi-Culti Foods-All-Ethnic

---

35. Drumming

+ For Dance
+ For Ritual Theatre
+ For Song
+ For Peace
+ For Joy

---

36. Re-enchanting Life with:

+ Mirth
+ Myth
+ Magic
+ Miracles
+ Mantras

---

37. Family Budget

+ Food
+ Lodging
+ Medicine
+ Transportation
+ Entertainment

38. Impulse Buying
+ Reading
+ Humanitarian Cooperation
+ Savings Accounts
+ Ritual Sacrifice
+ Take a Course in a New Interest/Choice

---

39. Combatting Negativity
+ Projecting Positive Deeds in the Media
+ Changing Bad Habits
+ Healthy Sexual Identities
+ Critical Thinking-and-Feeling Games
+ Work Songs

---

40. Healing AIDS/HIV
+ Pillows and Stuffed Toys for Children
+ Medicines
+ Letters Requesting Help from Pharmaceutical Companies
+ Houses for Orphans
+ Contraception

Making Suitable Choices

"War, battle, heartbreak, separation, pain. What do we gain from such tragedy? We are separated by our differences- yet our similarities are never attended.

Children, adults, people all around the world live in fear. War is not the answer. Why can't the differences be surpassed?

When you look at the world there is always a question that is unanswered–the question of peace.

The world is like open nature? There are always rough winds that stir up the hater, but in the end all is calmed down and is still beautiful."

© C.R. 14 years old, Montreal area high school

Behind Consumption and Consumerism Children as Consumers

Consider the following:

- **2 billion dollars** is roughly spent on advertising to young consumers in America, alone.
- The children's direct influence in parental purchases in the United States was estimated to be around **188 billion dollars** in 1997, up from $132 billion in 1990, $50 billion in 1984 and $20 billion in the mid-70s.
- The market for American children aged 4 to 12 years alone rakes in some **$30 billion dollars** annually.
- In the European Union, revenues to television networks and producers have reached between **$620 and $930 million.**

So what? Isn't that good for business? As we will introduce here, while this might be good for business, there are also important economic, social, health and environmental and other costs to be considered.

Encouraging and increasing childhood consumerism

The encouragement to have larger homes, more toys, and more "things" for children, as highlighted here by Richard Robbins, who is worth quoting at length:

The [U.S.] federal government played a major role in defining childhood. In 1929, Herbert Hoover sponsored a White House Conference on Child Health and Protection. The conference report, The Home and the Child, concluded that children were independent beings with particular concerns of their own. ... The report advised parents to give their children their own [furniture, toys, playrooms etc]. "Generally a sleeping room for each person is desirable", it noted. ...Take them shopping for their own "things and let them pick them out for themselves.

Through such experiences personality develops... [These] experiences have the advantage of also creating in the child a sense of personal as well as family pride in ownership, and eventually **teaching him that his personality can be expressed through things.** (White House, 1931, [Emphasis added by Robbins, 1999].

Thus in the space of some 30 years, the role of children in American life changed dramatically; they became, and remain, pillars of the consumer economy, with economic power rivaling that of adults" (Robbins, 1999, pp.24-25).

Children wield enormous purchasing power, both directly and indirectly (indirectly in the sense that they are able to persuade and influence parents on what to buy).

Observe a child and parent in a store. That high-pitched whining you'll hear coming from the cereal aisle is more than just the pleadings of a single kid bent on getting a box of Fruit Loops into the shopping cart. It is the sound of thousands of hours of market research, of an immense coordination of people, ideas and resources, of decades of social and economic change all rolled into a single, "Mommy, pleeease"

"If it's within [kids'] reach, they will touch it, and if they touch it, there's at least a chance that Mom or Dad will relent and buy it," writes retail anthropologist, Paco Underhill. The ideal placement of popular books and videos, he continues, should be on the lower shelves so the little ones can grab Barney or Teletubbies unimpeded by Mom or Dad, who possibly take a dim view of hyper commercialized critters (Cook, 2001).

Heavy advertising targeted at children

Heavy targeted advertising to children is for a reason! "Some $2 billion is spent annually to target juvenile consumers" in the United States, according to the MediaChannel (and the next quote says 1 billion alone is in the form of ads and commercials). Marketers see children as a future as well as current market and hence brand loyalty at a young age helps in the quest of continued sales later.

The Journal of the American Medical Association has said that children between the ages of two and seventeen watch an annual average of 15,000 to 18,000 hours of television, compared with 12,000 hours spent per year in school. Children are also major targets for TV advertising, whose impact is greater than usual because there is an apparent lessening of influence by parents and others in the older generation. …According to the [Committee on Communications of the American Academy of Pediatrics], children under the age of two should not watch television at all because at that age, brain development depends heavily on real human interactions. Nevertheless, $1 billion a year in spent on ads and commercials directed at children (Bagdikian, 2000, p. xxxvi).

In the European Union, revenues to television networks and producers have reached between **$620 and $930 million**. Sweden though, since 1991 has banned all advertising during children's prime time due to findings that children under 10 are incapable of telling the difference between a commercial and a programme, and cannot understand the purpose of a commercial until the age of 12.

European Union is now considering issues related to

advertising targeted at children and whether there should be a Europe-wide ban or regulation. Some complain that this industry provides jobs for people. Yet, this argument is weak, because it would be another example of "wasted labor", which is a waste of capital and waste of resources, and that labor could be used more effectively and efficiently elsewhere.

Corporatization of education

The education system in the USA, for example, has turned into a hugely profitable business estimated to be worth around $650 billion. From commercial-filled Channel One which many students must watch, sponsored and selective educational material, to commercialized school field trips the school system is bombarded by commercialism.

As well as children being targeted via the education system in the USA, as mentioned above, there is increasing concern at ad campaigns that are increasingly targeting children to be consumers and overly conscious about materialistic things, perhaps even at the expense of human qualities. One of the main reasons for such a fascination in children in this way is because of the potential purchasing power that children have. Zoll (2000) quoting from American Demographics of April 1988 stated:

> "In my practice I see kids becoming incredibly consumerist," said Kanner, who is based at the Wright Institute, a graduate psychology school in Berkeley, California. "The most stark example is when I ask them what they want to do when they grow up. They all say they want to make money. When they talk about their friends, they talk about the clothes they wear, the designer labels they wear, not the person's human qualities. In the 1960s, children aged 2 to 14 directly influenced about $5 billion in parental purchases," McNeal [professor

of marketing at Texas A&M University] wrote "In the mid-1970s, the figure was $20 billion, and it rose to $50 billion by 1984. By 1990, kids' direct influence had reached $132 billion, and in 1997, it may have peaked at around $188 billion. Estimates show that children's aggregate spending roughly doubled during each decade of the 1960s, 1970s, and 1980s, and has tripled so far in the 1990s."

A small example of effects of child consumerism

Candy and sweets are often put on stands in shops at the eye level of children. While it would be healthier to have foods, like fruits and vegetables in those places, the bright colors and packaging used to sell sweets are more likely to attract children's attention.

The dictum of consumerism and corporate capitalism dictates that social good comes through subtle greed and meeting demands of people. Yet, putting candy at the eye level of children creates a demand that otherwise may not have been there, or not have been there in as much intensity. Likewise, highly caffeinated soft drinks that are being consumed more and more, have negative health effects.

In a later section, we will see a deeper pattern of waste of which this is a part. That is, the sugar and related industries, such as confectionaries, soda drinks etc, expend many resources (natural resources, labor, capital etc) on something that is so costly to society (which requires spending even more resources to deal with those costs). Yet, within our current system, all these expenditures are counted towards GDPs! Hence, this waste is not recognized as it is built into our system!

And the influential impact on children provides a longer lasting effect that can continue these cycles.

"What is most troubling is that children's culture has become virtually indistinguishable from consumer culture over the course of the last century. The cultural marketplace is now a key arena for the formation of the sense of self and of peer relationships, so much so that parents often are stuck between giving into a kid's purchase demands or risking their child becoming an outcast on the playground. Children consumers grow up to be more than just adult consumers. They become mothers and fathers, administrative assistants and bus drivers, nurses and realtors, online magazine editors and assistant professors–in short, they become us who, in turn, make more of them. Childhood makes capitalism hum over the long haul" (Dan Cook, August 20, 2001).

But this is not the only example. For years, other companies have linked their foods to such schemes for educational or sports equipment for schools, such as a popular British potato chip (crisps) company. What they get for selling this is and future consumers. This has also been an example of controversial, which was unanimously condemned at a large teachers union conference.

Parental versus Corporate Influence.

Parents have a hard time providing guidance and influence on their children when there are so many conflicting influences from outside:

Kids not only want things, but have acquired the socially sanctioned right to want–a right which parents are loath to violate. Layered onto direct child enticement and the supposed autonomy of the child-consumer are the day-to-day circumstances of overworked parents: a daily barrage of requests, tricky financial negotiations, and that nagging, unspoken desire to build the life/style they have learned to want during their childhoods (Cook, 2001).

However, another aspect to this that makes it a challenge is also due to the fact that such consumption is ingrained into the culture, and the parents typically grew up with aspects of that culture themselves!

The children's market works because it lives off of deeply-held beliefs about self-expression and freedom of choice–originally applied to the political sphere, and now almost inseparable from the culture of consumption. Children's commercial culture has quite successfully usurped kids'boundless creativity and personal agency, selling these back to them–and us–as "empowerment," a term that appeases parents while shielding marketers.

Linking one's sense of self to the choices offered by the marketplace confuses personal autonomy with consumer behavior. But, try telling that to a kid who only sees you standing in the way of the Chuck-E-Cheese-ified version of fun and happiness. Kids are keen to the adult-child power imbalance and to adult hypocrisy, especially when they are told to hold their desires in check by a parent who is blind to her or his own materialistic impulses (Dan Cook, August 20, 2001).

Commercialization of childhood itself, of festivals etc.

Commercialization of public and religious holidays helps promote sales as well. Christmas time in numerous countries, such as the United States, sees a very high amount of consumerism.

The toy industry for example depends on Christmas quite a lot. The promotion of St. Nicholas/Santa Claus/Father Christmas and an almost benign factory (or workshop) of elves and so forth producing toys for free, was a boost to commercialize Christmas, especially for children.

The recent hype and success of Harry Potter, as well as other children's characters has led to further sales for toy manufacturers. But as well as perhaps bringing joy and fun to children, as a report from U.S.-based National Labor Committee says, for workers who have to make these toys, these can be "Toys of Misery".

> In 2000, U.S. toy companies spent $837 million on advertising. The companies do not want us to know or to think, just to buy. National Labor Committee, December 2001 (Emphasis Is Original)

Another example related both to children as well as the more general culture and media, is that of Disney, as mentioned on this web site's media ownership section.

> No one's really worrying about what it [advertising to children] is teaching impressionable youth. Hey, I'm in the business of convincing people to buy things they don't need" Business Week, August 11, 1997 (Robbins, 1999).

There might not be anything apparently wrong with businesses trying to make sales and profit. However, the effects of things like mass consumption, the intense advertising, and targeting to children and its emphasis over so many aspects of daily lives is of concern. That is, the effects of constantly buying things, while discarding older but often functioning things, increasing demands on the world's resources for this consumption, managing more waste, exploiting other people to labor over this, and so on. And all this while many still go hungry and poor because their lands are being used to export away food and other resources for producing products to be consumed elsewhere. It is in this way that the pressure and drive for profits has led to an over-commercialized consumerism, which has wider effects around the world and on the unseen majority peoples of the world, as we look at next.

References

Bagdikian, B. (2000). The Media Monopoly. Boston: Beacon Press.

Cook, D. (2001). Lunchbox hegemony; Kids and the Marketplace, Then & Now, LiP Magazine (on line), August 20, pp.1-8 www.lipmagazine.org. Retrieved January 19, 2006 from www.comm.uiuc.edu/faculty/Links/cookVita.rtf

McNeal, J. (1998). Tapping the three kids' markets. American Demographics, April, 1998, pp. 1-8,
Retrieved from http://www.findarticles.com/p/articles/mi_m4021/is_n4_v20/ai_20497111/pg_3 January 18, 2006. (Copyright Gale see article)

National Labor Committee. (2001). Toys of Misery; A Report on the Toy Industry in China.

Robbins, R. (1999).Global Problem and the Culture of Capitalism. Boston: Allyn and Bacon.

Shah, A. (2003). Encouraging and increasing childhood consumerism. Retrieved from: http://www.globalissues.org/TradeRelated/Consumption/Children.asp.
Also, http://www.globalissues.org/TradeRelated/Consumption/Children.asp?Print=True

Zoll, M. (2000). Psychologists Challenge Ethics of Marketing to Children, American News Service, April 5, pp. 1-6 Retrieved January 17, 2006 from http://www.mediachannel org/originals/kidsell.shtml

Some Background Information on People, Education Power, Profits, and Advertisement

"It is better to light a candle than to curse the darkness."

Eleanor Roosevelt

Oscar Peterson spoke up in the 1980s saying blacks used toothpastes and deodorants helping to swell coffers of the manufacturers. Eaton's was established a 100 years ago and everybody shopped there. In their later years a few token blacks were hired. Three years before they went bankrupt token blacks were used in display ads (States, 2006).

Minorities: Ads Still Portray All–White Society

The conventional wisdom about minorities in advertising goes something like this: In the bad old days, before the civil rights movement of the 1960s, minorities seldom appeared in mainstream media advertising. But the 1960s brought Awareness and Sensitivity, as well as Desegregation. Since then, minorities have taken their place alongside whites in the integrated world of advertising.

Well, you can't prove that by me. For the past three months I have been scrutinizing television and print advertising but I haven't seen many minorities, either alone or with white companions.

Sure, from time to time, you find an ad with a black or an Asian American. Occasionally there may even be a Hispanic or an Indian (meaning someone who looks the way the media feel Hispanics or Indians are supposed to look).

Ricardo Montalban sounds wonderful (and ethnically appropriate) proclaiming the romantic virtues of the Chrysler Cordoba (even though he had to put the accent on the wrong syllable). Actor James Hong has a sure hand with an American Express card. And I'm delighted that Houston Oiler quarterback Warren Moon can use the telephone as well as throw touchdown passes. But for the most part, advertising appears suspiciously like that same old segregated neighborhood that we knew before the 1960s supposedly brought us integration.

There are four notable exceptions. First, minority singers belting melodic sales pitches, Second, third, and fourth sports, food, and booze. Minorities may seldom be deemed proper for selling cosmetics or shampoo, but they sure can hype sneakers, hamburgers, and beer.

Is Anyone to Blame for the American Drop-out Rate?

A decade ago I reviewed research on dropouts for the U.S. Secretary of Education's Indian Nations at Risk Task Force. In that review (see Reyhner, 1992a, 1992b) I focused on mostly "school-based" reasons for students dropping out of school. My review indicated that in large impersonal schools, the perception teachers didn't care, passive teaching methods, culturally irrelevant curriculum, inappropriate testing, tracked classes, and schools not involving parents contributed to the relatively high dropout rate for American Indian and other minority students. I chose to focus on school-based reasons because I thought that those were the ones that policy makers and school officials could have some control over in contrast to home-based reasons that were out of reach of the schools, and I didn't want to "blame the victim."

However, it turns out I was too optimistic about making changes in schools to improve the chances of success for American Indian and other minority students as can be seen by the ongoing attacks on bilingual education and the increasing use of high stakes testing. I am thinking more and more that those of us who want minorities to achieve greater academic success are going to have to follow the lead of John U. Ogbu and focus more on what minority students, their parents, and their communities can do to promote academic success in spite of the negative aspects of many schools.

Ogbu (2003) has studied for three decades why some minorities do well in American schools and others do not. His most recent study is titled *Black American Students in an Affluent Suburb*. Here he focuses on trying to understand why middle-class Black students in a very well funded school district are not as academically successful as their middle-class White peers, including being underrepresented in Honors and Advance Placement (AP) classes. An anthropologist, Ogbu used interviews and classroom observations to examine the dynamics influencing students' academic performance.

Ogbu has found in his research that some minority groups are much more academically successful than others in American schools. He differentiates between voluntary (immigrant) minorities, including many Asian immigrants, who do well and involuntary minorities, including Blacks and American Indians, who don't do as well. Voluntary minorities see schooling as a path to economic advancement, while doing well in school was equated by some Black students with "acting White," and "once individuals exceeded the level expected of them, other Blacks in the community would begin to criticize them" (p. 209). Students with oppositional identities to White culture and schools tended to suffer academically while students with home cultures that were viewed as just different from the culture of the school could do quite well.

While Ogbu found some school-based reasons for black students below average performance, such as counselors having too many students to deal with to provide much individual attention, much of the challenge he finds is in the students themselves and their families. Some Black students did not know why they needed to learn math, and they "did not view their present schooling as a preparation for their future participation in the adult opportunity structure" (p. 167). Some students "naively assumed that regardless of how they did in school they would end up in or inherit the socioeconomic status as(sic) their parents" (p. 169).

Teachers could be found with low expectations for Black students, but the role of students in creating teacher expectations, high or low, can be overlooked. Ogbu found that "the attitudes and behaviors of some Black students were partly responsible for the teachers' low expectations" (p. 129). Black students did not raise their hands as much as White students and were more likely to come to class without having done their homework. Blacks students were more likely to be distracted from classroom academics than White students, and Ogbu found a "norm of minimal effort" among some middle and high school Blacks. "It was not cool to work hard in school or to be academically engaged" (p. 213). Other things were more important, including "consumerism" and sports. Consumerism led students from middle-class families to take part-time jobs so they could have cell phones, computer games, and stylish clothes, and athletics distracted students from academics. Ogbu's research confirmed other studies that found that "some Black students invested so much time in sports that they had little time for their academic schoolwork" and "for some students, playing sports was all that mattered" (p. 157). The media aggravates student's consumerism and obsession with sports, making "athletes, entertainers, drug dealers and their success, wealth, or reputations more visible than Black doctors, lawyers, and other professionals" (p. 164).

Ogbu found that some Black parents "did not perceive themselves as active agents in the education process… The role of parents is apparently limited to putting pressure on teachers to do their job of teaching well; that is, limited to pushing teachers and other school personnel to educate their children" (p. 236). Ogbu found "dismal" Black parent involvement both at school and at home. While there is a history of "collective mistreatment" shared by involuntary minorities, including American Indians, Hispanics, and Blacks, that influences their view of White people and White institutions, including schools, the mistrust engendered by this history can hurt students chances for doing well in school. The emphasis on discrimination, "on breaking the barriers in education and in the opportunity structure," led to ignoring "the behavior and attitudes that are conducive to school success" (p. 148).

Ogbu does not recommend minority students assimilate in order to be academically successful. He finds that minorities can accommodate to "White" schools without assimilating and that students can successfully learn and use Standard English, which is needed for school success, while continuing to speak their home and community language, whether it be a tribal language, Spanish, or Ebonics. The home and community language is an important part of the community's collective identity.

In a series of studies of American Indian college students, Terry Huffman (2002) found that students' collective identity is critical to their academic success. Indian students going to college often find little there with which to relate and suffer feelings of alienation. Some of these students quickly become disillusioned, seeing schooling as assimilation to White culture and dropping out. Others persist, drawing personal strength from their Native heritage and learning to relate to White culture, using their traditional culture as an anchor.

While it is a mistake to believe that schools today have no problems, it is also a mistake to believe that they are the total problem and that minority students are victims that can't individually fight and overcome the educational odds against them. In fact, when parents and community members hold teachers and schools, rather than themselves and their children, entirely responsible for their children's academic performance they play into hands of conservatives seeking to destroy public schools (Bracey, 2002).

Among other things, Ogbu recommends that minority communities take advantage of and promote organizations that support students' academic success. These include the American Indian Science and Engineering Society (AISES) and the Society for Advancement of Chicanos and Native Americans in Science (SACNAS). For example, as an antidote for all the sports and entertainment role models students see on television, the SACNAS Biography Project teaches students about Chicano/ Latino and Native American scientists and includes profiles of scientists, mathematicians, and engineers written at the middle and high school levels. It is online at http://sacnas.com/biography/

Presidential Candidates and the Nation

Tribalism in academics, politics, business, law, and religion make for strong loyalties amongst the protected group or class much to the exclusion of all other comers. How to break out of the mould is a complex yet not insurmountable problem if good will is present to alter the status quo. Change the politicians and give more business leaders' ethical training and monitoring might offer starting positions for cleaning up cesspools of corruption greed, and waste of public funds.

The political parties spent $600 million marketing their presidential candidates in 2004, but nothing has changed. In fact, we are worse off. This country belongs to the people every bit as much as it belongs to the corporations. This is an appeal for your solidarity, creativity, and generous financial support; to take back our economy and remake it with a human face. Look around us. The U.S. trade deficit will exceed $580 billion (a record $680 billion at end of 2004), said U.S. Reserve Chief, Alan Greenspan (2005) this year, with China alone accounting for $145 billion of the shortfall. We have lost 2.5 million good-paying manufacturing jobs in the last four years. Productivity of the American worker is up 12 percent over the last three years, but real household income is down 3 percent. On the other hand, corporate profits are up 17 percent, to over one trillion dollars. Chinese government officials have declared that China will be the "cheap wage manufacturing center of the world for at least the next 20 years." Automobiles are being assembled in North Korea under slave labor conditions by workers paid 10 cents an hour. Three hundred thousand white-collar jobs were outsourced last year, and this will only accelerate. Microsoft's outsourcing to

India has grown 25 fold in the last three years. It does not have to be like this. We have a plan to fight back. But we can only do this together. The economy and jobs remain the number one concern for the American people. But many people are confused. They have no idea that corporations have demanded and won all sorts of enforceable laws-intellectual property and copyright laws backed up by sanctions-to protect their products. If you imitate Wal Mart's Faded Glory label, or the Nike Swoosh, or Disney's Mickey Mouse, you will go to prison and pay large fines. This is all overseen by the WTO. So the label, the trademark and the product are all protected. However, when you ask these same corporations: "Can't we also protect the basic rights of the 16-year-old girl who made the product?" They respond: "No, that would be an impediment to free trade." So we allow a system where the product is protected but not the human being who makes it. When it is clearly laid out, the vast majority of the American people see this as outrageous and morally indefensible. This is a real issue of moral values. Remember when the Burlington Coat Company was caught using dog and cat fur on its collars? People were so upset that we quickly passed laws to prohibit the import of dog and cat fur into the U.S. We did the right thing to protect dogs and cats in China. Now, why can't we do the same thing to protect the rights of human beings? We are the largest economy in the world. Imagine if the American people stood up and said to the corporations: "Fine. We will buy your products. But you cannot bring goods into the United States or sell them if they were made by children, or by forced labor, or by teenagers forced to work grueling shifts for pennies an hour-or by any exploited worker denied his or her rights" (NLC, 2005; Reyhner, 1992). Yeah! So, say all of us with all due respect to national sovereignties worldwide.

References

Bracey, G. (2002). The war against America's public schools: Privatizing schools, commercializing education. Boston: Allyn & Bacon.

Chan. A. (2005). French riots film. Retrieved January 26, 2006 from http://www. usatoday.com/tech/gaming/2005-12-15-french-riots-film_x.htm

Cook, D. (2001). Lunchbox hegemony; Kids and the Marketplace, Then & Now. LiP Magazine (on line), Aug. 20. Retrieved November 4, 2005 from http://www.lipmagazine.org.

Cortes, C. (2000). The Children Are Watching: how the media teach about diversity. New York: Teachers College Press.

Greenspan, A. (2005) U.S budget deficit could disrupt global economy: Greenspan. The Gazette, Montreal, Saturday, December 3, p. B18.

Huffman, T. (2001). Resistance theory and the transculturation hypothesis as explanations of college attrition and persistence among culturally traditional American Indian students. Journal of American Indian Education, 40, 3, pp. 1-23.

McChesney, R. (1999). Rich Media, Poor Democracy: Communication Politics in Dubious Times. Urbana: University of Illinois Press.

McChesney, R. (2000). The Merchants of Cool. Retrieved October 11, 2005 from http://www.pbs.org/cgi-registry/stationlink.cgir

McPherson, W. (1984). Testing The Current. New York: Simon & Schuster. 1984).

Ogbu, J. (2003). Black American students in an affluent suburb: A study of academic disengagement. Mawah, NJ: Lawrence Erlbaum.

Reyhner, J. (2003). Is Anyone to Blame for the American Drop-out Rate? Indigenous Education NABE News Columns 2000, 26, 6, 26-27, July/August 2003. Retrieved April 3, 2005 from https://www.paypal.com/xclick/business=ssarkar%40nlcnet.org&item_na me=Working+to+End+Sweatshops+%26+Child+Labor&no_shipping=1&retur n=http%3A//www.nlcnet.org/thanks.shtml&no_note=1&tax=0&currency_ code=USDC © 1995-2005 National Labor Committee.

Reyhner, J. (1992a). Plans for dropout prevention and special school support services for American Indian and Alaska Native students. Retrieved June 9, 2003 at http://jan.ucc.nau. edu/~jar/INAR.html

Reyhner, J. (1992). American Indians out of school: A review of school-based causes and solutions. Journal of American Indian Education, 31(3), 37-56. Retrieved June 9, 2003 at http://jaie.asu.edu/v31/V31S3ind.htm

Schor, J. (2003). The Stepford Kids Born To Buy: The Commercialized Child and the New Consumer Culture By. New York: Scribner.

States, V. (2006). A personal note.

Toys of Misery; A Report on the Toy Industry in China, National Labor Committee, December 2001.

Conclusion

The Revitalisation of Daily Living

Conjure up your talents to bring imagination, play, and creativity back to healthful livings based on independence, freedom, and respect for human dignity. For example, employ the Media Awareness Network Search Home For Teachers For Parents Media Issues News.

BACKGROUNDER
Buy Nothing Day – Teaching/Parent Backgrounder:
Buy Nothing Day Activities for the classroom and the home International Buy Nothing Day always falls on the day after the American Thanksgiving in November, traditionally the first day of Christmas shopping! People are encouraged to not make any purchases throughout the entire day. The idea is to increase participants' awareness of their spending habits and to think about mass consumerism and its effect

on the cultural and natural environment of the world. Here are some questions to explore with your kids and students. Do you think that we buy more things than we really need each day? Make a list of things which your family would normally spend money on each day for example, food, gas, bus fare, clothing etc. Do think your family could go for a whole day without spending any money? Discuss the relevance of discouraging consumerism when we live in a capitalist country. Would it be more appropriate to celebrate Buy Nothing Day by encouraging citizens to buy from local businesses rather than from stores owned by large multinational corporations? Look at your spending habits over the course of a month and see where most of your money goes. Do you attempt to budget your money? Talk about how our culture has changed from one where people had to grow their food, build their own homes and make their own clothing to one where we pay money for all those things. What things would the early pioneers have had to buy which they couldn't supply themselves. i.e. flour, cloth for clothing, china, pots and pans etc.? Why do we, as a culture, feel compelled to buy things we don't need for survival? Do you think commercials and advertisements makes us feel we need things when we really don't? Can you think of reasons why buying things could be necessary for our society? Does it help the economy? Does it hurt the environment?

Activities: Visit a pioneer village or a museum. Discuss how we have moved from being a rural population to an urban one and what repercussions this change has had on society and the environment. Have your kids make something from scratch–something they would normally buy, i.e. a loaf of bread, Christmas presents, etc. Have your kids to write a story or play around the theme of consumerism and youth. Create a "Buy Nothing Day" celebration at your school–hold a poster contest or a competition to see which class can come up with the best idea for promoting non-consumerism in your community. Related Lesson Talking Back Recommended reading, viewing, surfing (Adbusters, 2005).

Samples of Workshop Activities You Could Organize and Run in Your Community

Let the participants learn basic tools about
- Family economics, for example:
- Family budgeting, consumption behavior, (Make a list of the top 10 items that appear regularly on your weekly/monthly budget)
- Impulse buying, deferred vs. instant gratification, (role playing The "I simply must have that thing, feeling, or attitude or I will not talk to you ever again!" game (What major possessions or attitudes (3) would you give up to own that new article, product, or feeling?
- Investing vs. consuming (List 5 advantages of saving vs. consuming)

What object, activity, time, plan, place, or privilege do you most badly want to save for over the next 3 months?

You're always pinching pennies. Penny wise pound foolish. Let's save for the rainy day. How do you react to these sayings in positive ways?

Media Awareness Network

1. Making Your School a Commercial-free Zone School-
the school used to be a place where children were protected
from advertising and consumer messages; but not anymore.
Budget shortfalls are forcing school boards to allow corporations
access to students in exchange for badly needed cash, computers
and educational materials. Corporations know the school is a
powerful environment for promoting their names and products.
A school setting delivers a captive youth audience and implies
the endorsement of teachers and the education system. Use the
following tips for raising awareness and taking action on the
commercialization of education in your school community:

2. Develop a policy for your school or school board. Work
with your parent and student councils and school administrators
to develop guidelines and policies for commercialization and
corporate **partnerships in your school. If your school board or
district doesn't it have a policy regarding corporate involvement,
work with your trustees to encourage your board to create one.**

3. For examples of guidelines and policies on corporate advertising
and partnerships in schools, **see Guidelines for Education/
Business Partnerships** from the B.C. Teachers' Federation:
http://www.bctf.ca/parents/IssuesInEducation/Support/Guidelines.html

4. Hold an awareness raising event at your school. To
educate students and teachers about the issue of commercialization
of education hold a "logo-free day" event at your school. Do a
"commercialism walk-through" in which students make lists of the
corporate logos on display, including soda machines, sponsored
educational materials, etc. If your administration agrees, have

students cover up all the corporate logos in the school for one day.

5. Involve your local media. Write an Opinion Editorial (Op Ed) explaining the issues surrounding the commercialization of education and send it to your local daily newspaper and community newspapers. Invite a reporter to attend an awareness raising event at your school.

5. Support a strong public education system. Support political parties that endorse a properly funded public education system.

Lobby your provincial government for increased spending on education. Without proper funding school boards will increasingly be forced to look to the private sector for additional revenues and resources.

6. Promote media education in your school community. Students need to learn to think critically about marketing directed at them.

Teachers and parents should teach kids from an early age to understand when and how they are being marketed to.

7. Visit the Site Directory </english/tools/site_directory/index. cfm> for more on this topic You have *items* in your content cart

Your Family and Media
A Survey
A number of parents in our school are concerned about the impact media violence is having on our children. We want to try

to reduce its effects right here in our community and we believe there are many positive things we can do.

Please fill out this brief survey and help us determine just where our collective energy as volunteers should be spent to ensure the relationship our kids have with the media is a positive one. (Please answer these questions with your oldest child, attending this school, in mind.)

Name:
Age of child_____ **Male or Female**_____

Viewing Habits

1. How many hours does your child watch TV programs and videos per week? Less than 5hrs/ 5-10hrs/ 10-15hrs/ 15-20hrs/ More than 20hrs

2. Do you limit the amount of time your child watches TV or videos? Not at all/ A little/ Some/ A great deal

3. How many hours does your child play video games per week? Less than 5hrs/ 5-10hrs/ 10-15hrs/ 15-20hrs/ More than 20hrs

4. Do you limit the amount of time your child plays video games? Not at all/ A little/ Some/ A great deal

5. Do you restrict your child from watching certain videos or TV shows? Yes/ No   Why?_____
_____

6. Do you restrict your child from playing certain video

games? Yes/ No   Why?_____

_____

7. Approximately what percentage of your child's TV and video viewing per week is general programming, not children's programming (ie. news shows, adult sitcoms, talk shows etc.)? _____

_____

8. How much does violence in children's media concern you? Not at all/ A little/ Some/ A great deal

9. How much does gender stereotyping in children's media concern you? Not at all/ A little/ Some/ A great deal

10. How much does racial stereotyping in children's media concern you? Not at all/ A little/ Some/ A great deal *What can we do?*

11. Would you be interested in articles on the subject of children and media if they were made available through the school library or newsletter? Not at all/ A little/ Some/ A great deal

12. Would you borrow quality videos if a lending library were set up in the school/community centre (ie. donated educational or entertainment videos)? Not at all/ A little/ Some/ A great deal

13. Would you be interested in attending a media literacy workshop for parents?   Not at all/ A little/ Some/ A great deal?

14. Would you like more information on how to let your

views become known to broadcasters (i.e. examples of letters and addresses of appropriate contact persons)? Yes/ No

Kindly Make up 6 more of Critical Questions Important to Your Child's Media Interests and Needs:

15.

16.

17.

18.

19.

20.

Discover insights for managing stress and daily life. Discuss new nutritional attitudes and strategies while sharing personal experiences and motivation.

Advertisement

These are just a few of the many reasons why Schor believes that Corporate America has succeeded in a frightening, Stepford Wives–like takeover of tween consciousness. In her artfully argued, important exposé, Born To Buy: The Commercialized Child and the New Consumer Culture, Schor draws on interviews with marketers, academic research, and her own survey of Massachusetts fifth- and sixth-graders. Her chief villains: "predatory" marketers who go so far as to pay parents and schools to get access to kids.

Because kids have gotten so skeptical, companies have countered with more craftiness. They hire cool alpha boys to flack products to their pals. They find "It" girls to host slumber parties and then ply their friends with products.

Nowhere is the onslaught more apparent than on TV and the Internet, says Schor. Against the $15 billion lavished on commercials, "neuromarketing," and covert peer-to-peer campaigns, Schor believes grade-schoolers don't stand a chance. Marketers have sidestepped gatekeeper moms and dads and gone directly to kids: Much of their work in schools and on the Net is so stealthy that parents aren't even aware of it. Thus, Schor argues, too many children have been transformed into miniature consumption machines who keep swallowing the corporate message that meaning comes from acquiring and a sense of self-worth from owning. You don't have one? What a loser.

Michelle Conlin
PBS KIDS GO! Don't Buy It, Get Media Smart! Click Here
TRUCE: *T*eachers *R*esisting *U*nhealthy *C*hildren's *E*ntertainment

Who We Are

Teachers **R**esisting **U**nhealthy **C**hildren's **E**ntertainment is an organization of early childhood professionals that works to promote a positive play environment for children. We share a concern about how children's entertainment and toys affect behavior and learning. TRUCE produces written materials, such as the Toy Action Guide As a small, grassroots organization, we rely on the efforts of concerned professionals and parents, to help with the distribution of our materials.

We believe that toys should enhance children's natural ability to actively engage in imaginative and meaningful play. Toys should help children work on the central developmental issues of their age and be open-minded enough to allow children to bring in their own ideas and solve their own problems.

We also believe that media, a powerful force in children's lives, has negative effects when it reinforces stereotypes, promotes violence and bombards children with sexually explicit images. Our mission is to raise public awareness about the harmful influence of Unhealthy children's entertainment and to provide parents and educators with information about toys and activities that promote healthy play. We are working to eliminate marketing aimed at exploiting children and to reduce the sale of toys and entertainment that promote violence. We hope that you will copy and distribute our materials to help spread the word in your community.

TRUCE Steering Committee: (TRUCE, 2005) Campaign For A Commercial-Free Childhood (formerly Stop Commercial Exploitation of Children) is a national coalition of health care professionals, educators, advocacy groups and concerned parents who counter the harmful effects of marketing to children through action, advocacy, education, research, and collaboration among organizations and individuals who care about children. We support the rights of children to grow up–and the rights of parents to raise them–without being undermined by rampant consumerism (Commercial Free Adulthood, 2004).

Use your idiom, myth, mirth, magic, miracles, medicine, mantras, and –Go ahead! Involve your child in healthy, playful, communicative activities and moments that enrich life. Most importantly, listen, watch, and engage in their excitement, meaningful learning and utterances in connecting with where they travel on this journey of discovery. Good Luck!

Should you wish to communicate any of the wonderful, eventful, and life enhancing opportunities you've had to develop love, friendship, and understanding with your child or if you the reader wish to include me in your adventures, please contact me at:

Philip.Taylor@consumerismandkids.com
or at:
consumerismandkids.com
888 de l'Eglise, Montreal, Quebec H4G 2N2, Canada.

With thanks and looking forward to hearing from you.

References

Adbusters: Media Awareness Network Search Home. Retrieved October 14, 2005 from http://209.29.148.33/english/resources/parents_resources/handouts/handouts_family_survey.cfm> Réseau éducation-médias </francais/index.cfm>

Brunk, M. (1972). A talk before the Annual Meeting of the Cooperative Extension Association of Livingston County, New York, November 15, The Freeman, The Foundation for Economic Education, Inc., February 1973, 23, 2.

Buy Nothing Day Special Initiatives Content Cart Réseau éducation-médias Commercial Free Childhood (2004). Be Informed CCFC is a program of the Judge Baker Children's Center <http://www.jbcc.harvard.edu/ Copyright 2004. All rights reserved http://t.extreme-dm.com/?login=sceccom

Graydon, S. (2003). Made You Look: How Advertising Works. Annick Press: Toronto.

Kinsella, S. (2003). Confessions of a Shopaholic. New York: Dell Publishing

Quart, A. (2003). Branded: The Buying and Selling of Teenagers. New York: Perseus Book Groups.

Schor, J. (2004). Those Ads Are Enough to Make Your Kids Sick. Sunday, September 12, 2004; Page B04 Retrieved January 17, 2006 from http://www.washingtonpost.com/wp-dyn/print/sunday/outlook/

TEACHING Buy Nothing Day - Teaching Backgrounder: http://209.29.148.33/english/resources/educational/teaching_backgrounders/advertising_marketing/buy_nothing_day.cfm

Toy Action Guide TRUCE_Toy_Action_Guide_04-05.pdf> /Media Violence Guide Click here to download free Acrobat Reader software. http://www.adobe.com/products/acrobat/readstep2.html

TRUCE (2005). Teachers Resisting Unhealthy Children's Entertainment Home index. html/Toy Action Guide TRUCE_Toy_Action_Guide_04-05.pdf/ Media Violence Guide TRUCE_Media_Guide_04-05.pdf/Contact TRUCE

Your Family and Media survey. (2005). Retrieved 25 March, 2005 from http://www.mediaawareness.ca/english/resources/parents_resources/handouts/handouts_family_survey.cfm home to parents with your school newsletter.

www.ingramcontent.com/pod-product-compliance
Lightning Source LLC
Chambersburg PA
CBHW051337170526
45166CB00002B/846